DESIGNING AND MAKING
TABLEWARE
AT THE WHEEL

Catherine & Matt West

DESIGNING AND MAKING
TABLEWARE
AT THE WHEEL

THE CROWOOD PRESS

CONTENTS

	Introduction	7
1	Tableware Design	9
2	Technical Design Considerations	19
3	Clay Preparation, Throwing and Trimming Processes	29
4	Step-by-Step Making Processes	51
5	An Introduction to Glazing	75
6	Understanding Glaze Chemistry and Raw Materials	91
7	Firing Your Work	103
8	Experimentation and Creating Meaning	115
9	Creating a Studio Layout for Hand-Thrown Tableware Production	125
	Selected Glaze Recipes and Formulas	135
	Contributors and Suppliers	137
	Bibliography and Further Reading	138
	Glossary	139
	Index	142

INTRODUCTION

The relationship between the food we eat and the tableware on which it is served is fascinating. As both food-lovers and potters we see parallels between the two. Working with clay is about working with the earth and respecting the finite resources available. It is about embracing a slower pace of life with an emphasis on process rather than solely the end result, and it is about learning and repeating traditional techniques in a predominantly digital world.

For many of us, a vast amount of our time is spent in front of a screen; this digital landscape is replacing the physical one in which the skill of the hand and an intimate knowledge of our land is no longer a prerequisite for survival. We can easily find ourselves disconnected from the material world and the way in which objects are made; indeed, many things that we purchase are mass-produced at an industrial scale. In a general sense, many of us have forgotten how to use our hands.

Fortunately, in the past decade there has been a significant resurgence and revival of our heritage crafts, pottery being a popular one. Many of us turn to clay for its soothing, humbling qualities as an antidote to busy lives, creating functional pieces to use at home, especially if we are keen cooks. Designing, making and using our own tableware taps into something very human and primitive within us all.

This revival perhaps follows a monumental shift in the food world too, with most of us all too aware of the environmental chaos of food production and health crises world-over, where diet has come to rely on heavily processed food that is so damaging – not only to our health, but also to the environment and our cultures. As many people have returned to a process of 're-learning' the skills of the generations before us in food preparation, so too has a fresh appreciation for craft emerged in a whole new generation.

This is a cause for celebration. While reading this book you'll encounter two voices: my own (Catherine's) and my husband, business partner and fellow potter – Matt's.

We are a husband-and-wife team of potters, makers and designers and we've written this book together. Our studio, Pottery West, was established in 2015. Almost a decade on, we're now a team of three, keeping operations deliberately small scale and specialising in the design and production of wheel-thrown tableware using traditional techniques.

At university, I studied Fine Art and Matt studied Design, both at Goldsmiths, University of London. After a few years working as a professional designer after graduation, Matt made the decision to re-train as a baker, following his passion and increasing interest in the Slow Food Movement. During this time our combined interest in cooking led us to start collecting studio pottery, mainly wood-fired pieces from potters such as the late Richard Batterham and Svend Bayer, purchased through David Mellor Design in Hathersage. We started to visit pottery exhibitions, including the W.A. Ismay Collection, which was exhibited at the Hepworth Gallery, Wakefield, and I worked in promoting and marketing for craftspeople, followed by a marketing and writing position at an architecture firm. It did not take long for us to give throwing at the wheel a go. As they say, the rest is history.

Because our passion for pottery began with a love of food, we've always been proud to celebrate and specialise in the design and production of tableware at the wheel, as opposed to producing more decorative pieces. We are both largely self-taught in our craft, something that we think is important to say because pottery is a hugely technical and varied discipline. This book focuses on the areas in which we have learnt so much through practical trial and error, research and knowledge acquired through a generous and clever network of fellow potters over the years, and also many hours of dedicated study and practice. As a result, we hope that this book will provide a technical, personal and accessible instruction into the design and production of tableware at the wheel, a subject that is certainly a passion of ours, and hopefully will soon be yours too.

Plate, bowl and espresso cup in Pottery West's 'sand' glaze. (Photo: India Hobson)

CHAPTER 1

TABLEWARE DESIGN

The things we make and the pieces we choose to use in our everyday lives tell a story about who we are. If we look at the history of ceramic tableware, we can see a perfect honing of form and function, a process that has been percolating in delicate balance for thousands of years. From a simple vessel formed out of raw clay with only hands as tools, to a highly engineered piece created using industrial techniques in a factory, these processes and items reflect our society, our material knowledge and our food cultures. While many crafted objects turn to dust over the centuries, a great many pots survive, leaving behind fascinating clues into ancient ideas, practices and contexts.

Pottery is an ancient craft rooted in basic materials and human skill while also being extremely relevant to us today. There are so many techniques and skills that can be used to create pots, and innovative production methods are always in development. This book focuses on one mode of traditional tableware production – hand-thrown pottery. In this chapter we will outline a series of design considerations and tips to get you started with the design and production of your own hand-thrown tableware.

Working with our hands to create wheel-thrown tableware is a practical antidote to fast-paced living where we spend more and more time in front of computer screens.

A completed prototype of a batter bowl.

DESIGN CONSIDERATIONS

Sustainability

One of the overarching dilemmas with which we must engage is that the production of pottery isn't necessarily a sustainable process: by producing a pot we are using finite resources, often precious metals and minerals from the earth; once fired, it will be thousands of years before it will be returned to the earth as a useful material. Furthermore, we are using energy and water in the process, albeit on a small scale.

It is important to acknowledge this and consider, as the most fundamental design consideration, whether or not the piece really needs to be made in the first place. Will this be useful, will it have a place, does it need to use this particular material and is there a more efficient way of making this? Producing pottery in small batches at the wheel is hardly mass production, but it is still important to be a responsible producer.

There are many ways in which we can be more resourceful in the production process, which we will discuss in more detail throughout the book. Using a local clay and sourcing glaze materials that are abundant in your region is a good place to start. Some oxides and raw materials will inevitably need to be sourced from elsewhere but you can also consider how to incorporate waste materials into your work. Wood ash from a wood-wood-burning stove and waste glaze from tests can be incorporated. If you make something you are not happy with at greenware stage, be sure to recycle the clay rather than fire the pot. Developing methods to reduce firing times, using single firing and also making sure your electric kiln is powered by renewable energy are all good things to think about.

Form and Function

The relationship between man and earth is a complicated one, yet pottery encapsulates a harmony between the two that goes back to the beginning of civilisation. Its evolution follows a fascinating anthropological narrative. Rooted in a situation of pure function and circumstance, and becoming something more cultural and delicately balanced in our globalised society, hand-thrown tableware is just one small discipline under the expansive umbrella of ceramics. However, something specific to tableware is that it serves a function – it must be able to be drunk from, eaten off or cooked with.

The flecks in the glaze used on this jar are composed of 'waste glaze' from a phase of glaze testing. The spent glaze tests were dried, biscuit fired then added to an existing glaze. It is always worth thinking about ways in which precious raw materials can be used rather than discarded.

A batch of trimmed soup bowls drying on ware boards before being biscuit fired.

For many makers at the beginning of the journey into designing and producing hand-thrown tableware, the requirement to function can present itself an awkward inconvenience in the creative process. Playful ideas and special glaze effects are very seductive and it can be tempting to ignore the more pragmatic side of making. But once you get going and use some of your pieces, a more restrained voice begins to dominate. Your exquisitely elegant bowl with the tiny foot might be prone to toppling when full of food, for example, or the seductive matt glaze you're using for a mug might become tea-stained instantaneously. We would also add that as potters and designers, we don't want to diminish all creativity and playfulness for the sake of function. Hand-thrown tableware offers a double-edged sword: on the one hand it needs to function well; on the other, if it doesn't celebrate the character and craftsmanship of the maker and process then what is the point? Our biggest offering here is that humans are not machines; we have hands that feel and the objects we make are reflections of our time, circumstance and emotion. It's a balancing act of creating something functional and keeping those elements present in the work. Starting off with simplicity in mind, with the objective of improving skill and building a solid foundation of knowledge, will put you, the maker, in great stead for adding in character and playfulness as you progress.

Connection

Within the design process, one of the first questions to ask yourself is 'how do you want the user of your work to feel?' For example, do you want the shape of the mug to be comforting in the hand? Would you like the glaze to feel a certain way? Do you want to create a feeling of calm, or are you hoping for elegance or opulence? There isn't a right or wrong answer but it is a very useful exercise to begin with. Once you understand your desires for a piece it will be easier to make technical decisions later on.

Functionality and Purpose

In most cases the function of a pot will, if not dictate, suggest the form. Think about the food type that will be served in a bowl, for example, or the types of drink to be had from a particular sized mug. Because you are designing and making pieces to be used it is vital to interrogate whether or not your work is fit for purpose. Use the piece yourself

The gently tapering lip of the bowl is an intentional design decision as well as an aesthetic one, enabling the user to walk easily with bowl in hand without spilling the contents.

and ask friends and family to also test out prototypes before committing to a final design.

Durability

Hand-thrown tableware is inherently bound to have more inconsistency in its making than industrial techniques of production. Having said that, if pieces are looked after and cared for there is nothing to say a well-used pottery piece can't be passed down as an heirloom. Using stoneware or porcelain and firing to cone 10 (*see* Chapter 7 for more about firing) while using a well-fitting and durable glaze creates the strongest tableware. It is absolutely possible to make tableware using earthenware (indeed, in Britain we have a great heritage in this), but a greater level of technical expertise is required, which we will cover in later chapters.

Most people use a dishwasher and handmade pottery can be compatible with this, although dishwashers can be very abrasive. We would always encourage people to care for their ceramics by hand-washing but also understand that it isn't always practical, especially in a restaurant setting. In Chapters 5 and 6, we will talk more about how to create a durable glaze.

Efficiency in Making

Hand-thrown tableware is often produced in small batches and so it is prudent to consider whether elements of your design are repeatable and whether they can be scaled up. There is an inherent time pressure when it comes to working with clay. As the clay begins to dry, the window of opportunity closes for attaching components, such as handles and spouts, without the risk of cracks appearing. You may also want to think about the time something takes in terms of cost and failure rate. Where there is a problem there is a challenge and usually a design solution that leads to new innovate findings. It is always good to embrace the problem head-on rather than ignoring it.

Take note of how long the processes are taking you for a batch so that you have an accurate record for later, should you wish to establish a price for selling.

Colour and Texture

Many potters at the beginning of learning their craft focus heavily on the throwing aspect and therefore the form. But it is important to think about glaze at the outset.

A small batch of pourers being assembled.

An assortment of different glazes and tableware forms.

Unfortunately, this isn't always straightforward and takes some trial-and-error work and therefore time. For example, a bowl that looks great in one glaze colour might just not work well for a mug. A dark, semi-matt glaze might help food with colour 'pop' in a restaurant setting, but for something more domestic, perhaps a paler and cleaner glaze would be more appealing. Colour is very subjective and different people favour different things. It is important that you work within your own design objectives and tastes rather than allowing other people's influence or trends to dominate your choices.

As well as colour it is useful to consider texture. Glazes can be glossy, matt or satin and special effect glazes can be intentionally crawled, crazed (*see* Chapter 5), crystalline or volcanic. Normally we wouldn't be using special effect glazes for any pieces intended for food, but occasionally, if working with a concept-driven restaurant, for example, we might incorporate some of those elements so long as the function upholds.

Learning from the Past

We can benefit by studying historically validated archetypal forms by other potters. Our museums and libraries offer a wealth of information and design resource. It's good to question why different forms, styles and glazes were used in certain geographies and contexts. What type of food did this hold? What does the delicate foot of the pot say about the owner of this vessel? Don't be afraid to follow the lead of the potters that have gone before you as a primary form of inspiration; it isn't plagiarism. After all, with a craft as ancient as pottery, much of the trial-and-error work of developing forms has already been done by others and it would be foolish to disregard that. But rather than imitate, think whether or not it relates to our present-day context and whether an element can be challenged and improved.

A Slow Craft

Many potters talk about their process being a slow one and how it is not easy to create an economically efficient practice (particularly when making thrown tableware as opposed to display pots). I like to take these negative attributes and flip them on their head. Slowness is a guiding principle; taking your time to make this labour-intensive

Embracing the slow and repetitive nature of making tableware by hand is important. Here is a teapot being assembled carefully by hand.

product to the best of your skill is an antidote to a time-obsessed culture.

THE DESIGN PROCESS

Questioning

At the outset of a project, it is useful to have a discussion with the client or end user, if applicable, about their expectations of the piece. If not for a client but for a personal project, ask yourself these questions or even include a friend in the discussion. How is this piece going to be used? Who is going to use it? How do you want them to feel? How will it be cared for in terms of washing and storing?

What temperature does it need to withstand? How big does it need to be in terms of scale and capacity? How many need to be produced? Is there a particular typology for this form, for example a tea bowl, and how does that relate to a particular culture? Does this piece need to be made on the wheel rather than by other processes that may be more appropriate?

Drawing at the Wheel

Drawing is so important. It helps get the ideas out of your head and into something that is tangible. We find sketching ideas for shapes to be a really useful exercise before committing something into clay. Having said that, drawing can only take us so far and there is an element of 'sketching at the wheel' to be done to help understand ideas three-dimensionally. Once you have a notion of shape and size it can be useful to go ahead and throw some forms at the wheel, treating them as three-dimensional sketches.

After assessing these ideas, you can then go on to making prototypes. We would recommend producing at

Three different prototypes for a mixing bowl design. These have been thrown and trimmed but not yet fired and so can be recycled as needed.

least three options even if there are only subtle differences between them. At this point, think about scale, weight of clay, shrinkage, the limitations of the clay and also your skill levels. You can finish these prototypes – but not fire them – and analyse the shapes, breaking down any you don't want to pursue and reclaiming the clay.

If producing for a client, this is a good time to take photographs and communicate your ideas in order to gain feedback before going too far down one particular design path. As potters, we are fortunate that our material is infinitely recyclable until the point that we fire the clay, so we can experiment with form without creating too much waste.

Material Exploration

Once you've answered the initial questions and have sketched ideas in both pen and clay, it is worthwhile thinking about materials. You don't always have to use the same clay body although there are benefits to using a body; you have sound knowledge of when it comes to things like glaze fit and shrinkage. You might like to investigate, for example, using a

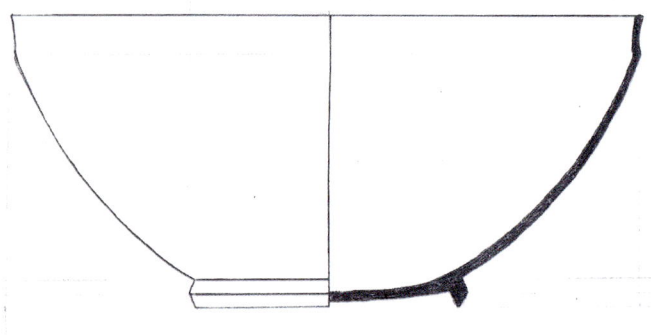

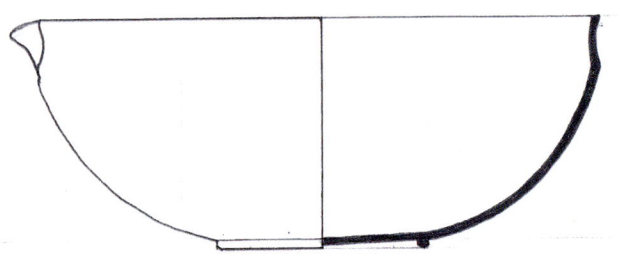

Initial pen sketches of a mixing bowl and batter bowl.

Glaze test tiles and raw materials. When working on a new design, I like to keep swatches and materials together in one place.

local clay, found raw materials, or non-ceramic components for things like handles, lids or trays. At the beginning of the project, start to create test tiles of glaze swatches and material samples. If you have success from your test tiles, scale them up and test on larger pieces to see how the glaze works on different shapes. Store all your findings in a box, container or on a shelf so everything is in one place. Keep notes and take photographs as you go. Apart from anything else, I find keeping all of this information in one place to be mentally stimulating and encouraging at points when you might feel stuck or unsure about the project.

Acknowledging the limitations of both material and evolving skills is important. Often we have an idea of what we'd like to produce, but the clay might not be the right material for this idea or it requires a great deal of skill to achieve. Retain a humble but ambitious approach, remembering that pottery is a lifelong journey of discovery and that success will come over time and not always instantaneously. However, this doesn't mean that we can't try and it doesn't mean we can't adapt our designs to work for us in the current chapter of our own particular making story.

It might be a cliche but the best way to learn and improve is to fail; this is certainly true when working with clay. Push the clay and your skills to the limits and then examine the results.

Test and React

Pottery is a slow process and it can be very tempting to rush or even skip the testing phase, especially when working to a deadline. Try to allocate enough time and headspace to really interrogate your prototypes. Take the piece home, use it intensively and ask yourself the questions you started with. Try to answer honestly and embrace any failures as important developmental milestones rather than negativities. If you are working alone, include others in this process and get some feedback. Take ownership over the design and making decisions rather than incorporating every suggestion into your design.

Sometimes there are things that go wrong in the making process, such as lids warping, cracks in handles and glazes that have too much movement and drip onto kiln shelves. The good news is that, with patience, knowledge and testing, it can potentially all be fixed for future pieces. The bad news is that it can take a long time and there can be headaches along the way. We hope that much of the information required will be found in the following chapters of this book, but sometimes a problem can be so persistent it is a good idea to leave it for a while, move on to something different and return again with fresh energy.

How we react at this stage is important. As a piece becomes more refined in the design process, it's often the subtle changes that enhance the character and success of the pot. Could you change the way the base of the pot is trimmed? Does the handle need to be higher or lower? Could the shape taper slightly, and so on? Sometimes these subtle alterations happen over a series of years.

Making a Batch

Once you've gone through the testing process and perhaps even produced some new prototypes, it is time to make a small batch. This is important because it will tell you how possible it is to repeat a form and scale up for small batch production. Often very small tweaks and developments happen gradually over time from batch to batch. This is because, over time, skills and knowledge develop and the maker might realise an easier or more advanced way of making. Accept this inevitability and go with it. Make a note of how long this first batch takes to make. It isn't always easy to record times as there are so many small jobs to include from clay preparation right through to fettling and firing, but try to be as accurate as possible. By making a batch rather than just a one-off, you can see if you speed up as you work. Often muscle memory kicks in quite quickly and you find that you speed up a little as you work. This aspect is less important if you are making for a personal project, but if you are needing to price the work, you'll want to know how much labour goes into the piece.

Technical Drawing

Once you are happy with the prototype, it is a good idea to commit your final design to a technical drawing. All of this work can be intensive but it is so easy to lose all of your

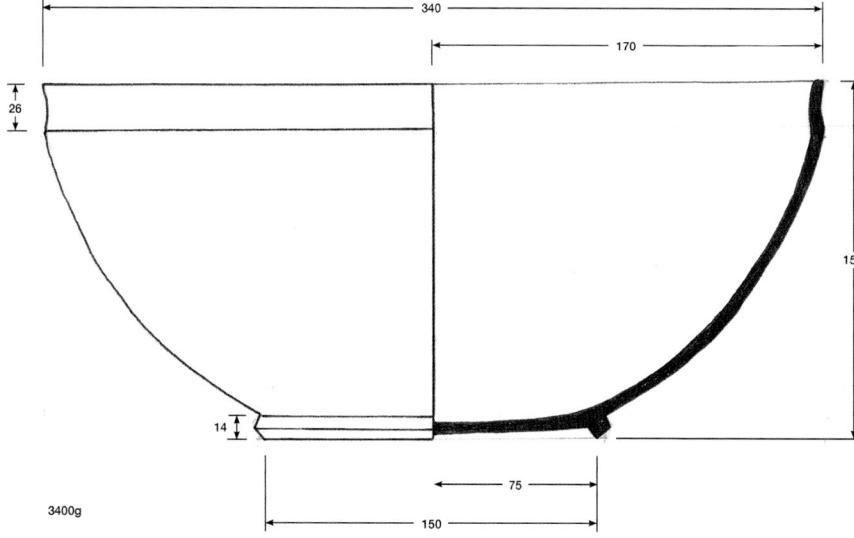

A technical drawing of the final design for a mixing bowl. Information to be included on the drawing consists of the weight of the clay, and the dimensions of the bowl to be thrown to and trimmed. You can also include glazing and other notes on this technical drawing.

technical information as projects move on, only to return to the form a year or so later and have to rely on memory. The technical drawing can either be created by hand or on a computer. Include the necessary information that you'll need to reproduce the piece, that is, the weight of clay thrown with, shrinkage rate (*see* Chapter 2), height and diameter, and trimming notes.

AUTHENTICITY, INTEGRITY AND CULTURAL APPROPRIATION

Designing and making wheel-thrown tableware in a studio pottery context can present some complexities in terms of ownership of the design. This is not only a design process; it is one of craftsmanship, process and skill. Furthermore, certain form typologies are universal and ancient and so no one potter can claim ownership or copyright over them. Potters can be protective about their glaze recipes but it is always good to remember that no two potters, even using the same glaze formula, will have the exact same outcome as there are so many variables in the making, from origins of raw materials, to firing cycles and glaze application.

It is not a coincidence that the works of many potters, especially when just starting out, bear aesthetic similarities to others. It is not a bad thing to imitate, particularly in the early stages of learning about throwing at the wheel. But as you progress and become more skilled, it is important to be mindful of this aspect. If looking at the work of other potters and peers for inspiration, be sure to acknowledge it to yourself. Look at their work analytically as well as emotionally and question what it is that works so well about their pieces and what doesn't. Compare this to your own matrix of design considerations. Include these pieces in a mood board if you like but be sure to separate and distinguish them from your own drawings. In our own studio, when we're working on new designs, we often 'mute' other potters on social media so that we are not even subconsciously influenced by their work. It sounds extreme, but it is very easy to be influenced, even at a subconscious level, by fashions and trends rather than what you know to be true to your design aspirations.

Cultural Appropriation

Pottery is rooted in the history of all nations and certain forms and styles are particularly ingrained into food cultures. Many Western potters take influence from Japanese and Korean pottery for instance. Be sure to honour the principles in which the originals were created. Educate yourself about the culture, explore, visit and be sure to understand the intricacies of that principle. In recent years, nuanced and difficult-to-articulate concepts such as 'wabi-sabi' have been used to name and sell Western products that miss the mark of the original impetus. Inspiration is always valid but appropriation isn't, even with your best intentions. If you're ever unsure, it may be good to talk it through with a friend – even better if you can involve someone from the culture in which you are referencing.

Finding Your Visual Identity

One of the most difficult things is to establish a visual identity with your pottery. Take comfort from the fact that, like most things, this takes time. In the early days, much of the learning is about technique, but once you have some skills under your belt you're probably going to be entering a phase of experimenting and making many types of form, glazes and firing techniques. This is excellent, healthy and essential. Make sure you take a step back now and again to observe which of these styles makes you happy and proud. What do you enjoy making? Is there something fascinating about the process that you would like to research further and does it spark ideas? You'll know when you are onto something good, and at this point try to pare down your output so you have a small selection of forms, glazes and techniques to follow. Taking the time to develop one or two signature pieces, such as a mug that is overtly yours, is well worth it.

CHAPTER 2

TECHNICAL DESIGN CONSIDERATIONS

Now that we've covered some design principles, it is time to go into more technical detail, considering techniques and design interventions we can implement directly into the making. Chapters 3 and 4 cover practical step-by-step guides to many of the forms and techniques described in this current chapter.

THE FOOT

Observe any potter encountering the work of another potter and most likely they will pick up the pot and examine the base of the pot carefully. The care and attention paid to the foot of the pot speaks volumes about the design intentions of the potter and is one of the first things to think about when creating a new form.

Consider how the glaze will work with the trimmed form, both aesthetically as well as practically. If you have a glaze with lots of movement, it can be a good idea to trim a line before the footing (5a and 5b in the image) to break the flow of the glaze.

When making forms such as plates, multiple foot rings can provide support to prevent the plate from slumping or warping during the firing.

A bevelled edge on the foot-ring (6a and 6b) can create an effect of weightlessness, almost as if the pot is hovering above its surface. Meanwhile, no foot-ring at all (1a and 1b) can provide a more rustic aesthetic, as well as being quicker

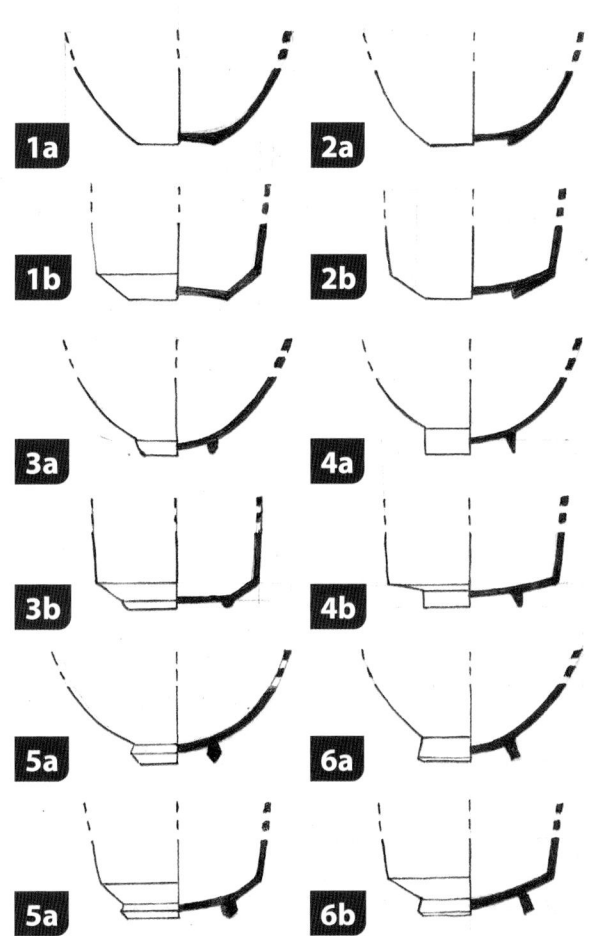

Cross-section drawings of different foot profiles. The detail of the foot can say a lot about your design intentions for a piece and impact the weight and balance both aesthetically and physically.

Using a calliper tool to measure the diameter of a teapot lid.

to produce. To take weight out of a pot without altering the aesthetic, you can create a hidden foot-ring (2a and 2b).

The pot always needs to be sitting on a point rather than one flat surface, so even if a pot doesn't have a foot-ring, it is always trimmed or even pressed to have a very slightly concave base so that it won't wobble.

Often, when designing a piece, the base of the pot within the foot-ring is carefully thought out in terms of shape and size to echo the interior form of the pot. This helps with balance and weight both physically and aesthetically.

MAKER'S MARKS

Most potters develop a signature to mark their work with. Like an artist's signature, it provides provenance and authenticity. There are few rules when it comes to the method and style of the mark, or indeed, whether to have one at all. It is relatively straightforward to carve your own mark – porcelain is a good material for this due to its strength – or you can also submit your design and purchase a laser-cut stamp. Other methods include writing or brushing with oxide or using a decal transfer.

On this pot we've used both a maker's mark and iron oxide to date the wood firing in which the piece was fired. Wood firings can be unpredictable (and therefore special) and so we thought it would be a good idea to date the piece.

An example of a maker's mark on the foot of a pot, this time placed on the lower tapered and unglazed foot rather than the base.

The foot of this bowl has a bevelled edge to create one fine point upon which the pot sits on a surface. It also lifts the form slightly, giving an impression of being lighter in weight.

An example of marking the foot of a pot with the maker's mark and a client logo.

Consider the placement of your stamp, and how subtle or noticeable you would like it to be. If you are producing a piece in collaboration with a client or restaurant, it might be that they would like their logo on the form somewhere also.

CLAY AND GLAZE CHOICES

While we discuss this in more detail in other chapters, the colour and texture of your finished piece are of course some of the biggest technical design aspects you will consider. It is almost impossible to consider the clay body without also considering the glaze, as the two are so interlinked with needing to fit together. It is also really important not to only think of the form and then consider the glazing later, as to create a really cohesive piece, it all needs to be considered as one. For example, a glaze that is very fluid will require attention as to where it should be glazed up to and whether it should be used on a vertical surface. Some glazes just don't work as well on different forms and so this needs to be tested in the prototyping stages.

A plate with the majority of the base glazed, with the exception of the foot-ring and maker's mark.

CLAY SHRINKAGE

Many people do not realise just how much clay shrinks in the making process as water evaporates from the clay in the drying process and then again in the firing process. It is not uncommon for a new potter to throw their perfect bowl only to find the fired version being so much smaller, as if it had shrunk in the wash! Most stoneware clay bodies have a shrinkage rate of approximately 12 per cent (and this varies a lot between clays). The shrinkage rate will be specified by the clay manufacturer but you can also calculate shrinkage yourself by measuring the pot at different points in the process – freshly thrown, green, bone dry, biscuit fired and glaze fired (see Chapter 7 for firing). Another good system is to create a clay 'ruler', which once fired should have a different 'one centimetre' than the original, by which you can establish the shrinkage rate.

FORMS

Plates

It is impossible to consider the subject of hand-thrown tableware without examining one of the most functional of forms: plates. Plates can present a great challenge

> **DESIGN CONSIDERATIONS**
>
> 1. Will this plate be used as a decorative piece or be eaten from?
> 2. What type of food will be eaten from it? For example, desserts, main meals or foods with sauces?
> 3. Is this an everyday plate or something that is used only for special occasions?
> 4. Will it be cleaned in a dishwasher?
> 5. Does it need to fit in a plate rack?
> 6. How many plates can you fit in your kiln? How many plates can you fit on one kiln shelf? This will enable you to assess the sizes you are comfortable with making.
> 7. Does your clay tend to slump during the firing? Do you need to create extra footings to support the base, or perhaps have no footings at all?
> 8. Glazes are often a little different when on flat forms, especially if they are less fluid – do you need to alter the glaze chemistry to accommodate this?

Hand-drawn diagrams of three plate typologies. The top plate has a rim and an outer and inner foot-ring to prevent slumping during the firing process. The middle plate is a flat-based plate with a vertical rim. The bottom plate has a continuous curve with two bevelled foot-rings.

to the potter. They are not particularly tricky to throw, but achieving consistency, preventing problems such as cracking, warping and slumping, and the amount of space required to fire them, are all potential headaches. Many professional potters don't make and sell plates for all of the above reasons.

Decoration, Alterations, Glazing and Finishing

When it comes to the glazing and decoration aspects of plates, much consideration should be taken as to the functionality and aesthetic of the design. With such a flat and wide surface area to work with, you may find that the glazes you use for other forms, such as mugs, appear slightly differently on a plate. Because it is likely that the user of your plate will be using cutlery, it is a good idea to test the impact that has on your glaze. Some glazes, especially ones using zirconium – which is commonly used to make white glazes – are more prone to cutlery marks, and scratches can also appear over time. Attention should be paid to the texture of the glaze also; some people have an aversion to the sound and feel of cutlery on a matt surface. With time, you'll get to know the intricacies of your glaze/form relationship. There are other methods of decoration too, including slip-trailing, sgraffito and using oxide washes, just to name a few.

Bowls

This is one of the most ancient of forms, since our relationship with clay goes back to something intrinsic between food and the earth, and within that functional parameter there is a great deal of creative opportunity. Bowls are such an everyday hyper-functional form that there are so many possible variations. Bowl typologies are synonymous with different food cultures and this is often a good place to begin your research. Apart from the obvious functional, cultural and aesthetic considerations, there is a great deal of freedom to be enjoyed when it comes to designing and making a bowl at the wheel.

DESIGN CONSIDERATIONS

- Is the bowl for food or display?
- What type of food will be eaten from it? Soups, desserts, ramen and so on?
- What size does it need to be?
- How is it to be held and/or carried?
- Is there a cultural association attached to this form?
- Will it be cleaned in a dishwasher?

Examples of different bowl forms but all with the same characteristics of having a rim, rounded bowl shape and foot. This is an example of exploratory prototyping to interrogate function and aesthetic.

A stack of glazed 'enclosed bowls'. These bowls are designed to be used for soups, stews and broths. They hold liquid well and the enclosed lip helps to create a feeling of containing the liquid.

Drinking Vessels

Mugs, cups, beakers, tea bowls – these can be thrown in the same way as a bowl or cylinder. There are a few things extra to consider, especially as people tend to be very particular about the vessels from which they drink.

DESIGN CONSIDERATIONS

- Which drink is the vessel for – tea, coffee, water, wine and so on?
- What size does it need to be?
- How is it to be held and/or carried?
- Is there a cultural association attached to this form?
- Think about the glaze – some people dislike very matt surfaces to drink from, for example, and some surfaces are more prone to staining.
- What kind of thickness would you like the walls to be. Does it need to retain heat for a long time?
- How does the thickness of the rim feel to drink from?
- How can the design help to keep the drink warm? Will very thin walls mean more heat loss?
- Will it be cleaned in a dishwasher?
- What kind of handle, if any, does the vessel need?
- What capacity does it need to have? Capacity can be really important; make sure you incorporate clay shrinkage rates into your design.

These bowls were made as part of an exploratory exercise, taking the same weight of clay and thrown to the same shape and dimensions but then altered to create six variations.

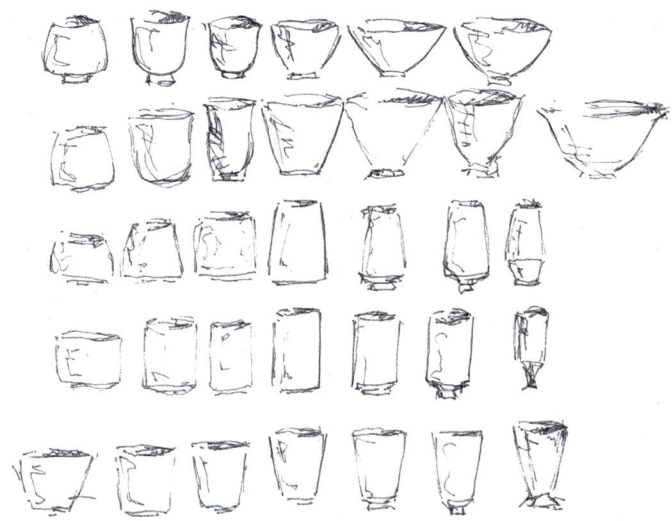

Hand-drawn exploratory sketches of different drinking vessel forms, all without handles.

Chapter 2 – Technical Design Considerations

Three wood-fired cups glazed in a celadon-type glaze. These can be used for a range of drink types.

Straight-sided mugs with pulled handles. The cylindrical form is deceptively difficult, since there is little to hide behind if the cylinder is not thrown perfectly.

Two types of handle can be seen here. Pulled handles on the mugs and a pulled top handle on the teapot.

An example of a finger-pulled spout on a bowl form.

Handles and Spouts

Not only do handles and spouts add functionality to a pot, they also enrich the character of a piece and can reflect the personality of the potter. Handles offer a point of contact between the hand of the user and the hand of the maker, especially a handle that has been pulled from the pot and formed through the shape of the potter's hand.

There are two main practical functions of a handle in tableware: to enable a vessel that is containing hot contents to be picked up, or if on a vessel such as a jug, to allow for an easy (usually one-handed) pouring action. These functions need to be considered when designing and making a handle. Slight variations in placement and shape can have a large impact on how a user may interact with the pot. For

A teapot spout, thrown at the wheel, cut and attached to the body when leather hard.

example, the placement of a handle on a jug containing a litre of water can affect how easy it is to pour, and balance when tipping.

Handles can be pulled, coiled, extruded, cast or built. In our studio, we favour pulled handles for their strength and versatility but there is a lot of room for experimentation. Within this method of pulling handles, there are many aesthetic variations.

A successful spout must be able to deliver a controlled flow of liquid with little or no drips or dribbling. (I am relatively relaxed about a spout leaving a drip or two of liquid behind once poured, but much more than that I see as a failure. I certainly don't want a spout to allow liquid to run back down the outer surface of a pot or drip while being poured from.)

There must therefore be a balance between design aesthetics and functionality. When designing a form with a handle and/or spout, a combination of initial drawings, prototyping and testing is important. Due to the nature of producing pottery, this can be a frustratingly slow process and requires patience. To speed things along, prototype in batches, making slight variations from piece to piece.

A pourer with a straight-sided handle and U-shaped spout, which was thrown and attached at the leather-hard stage.

Lids

Lidded forms are very pleasing to the potter but can be troublesome because a great deal of attention is required to make them fit well. The type of lid you choose to make depends on the functional requirements of the finished piece. For example, a lid on a teapot should stay relatively firmly in place so it doesn't slide off when pouring, but a lid on another form that is more decorative may not require as great a degree of accuracy.

DESIGN CONSIDERATIONS

- What is the function of the pot – does the lid need to be held in place while being tilted? If so, consider a lid with a deep flange and/or a gallery that the lid sits inside.
- Warpage can be a problem. Can the lid and pot be dried and fired together? This will reduce chances of the clay warping.
- Does the lid need to be fitted snugly? This dictates how you make the pot. Making the lid to measure specifically to each pot aids this, but if you want to make in larger quantity, more quickly, it is easier to create a batch of lids to one set measurement, which may mean the lids have a looser fit. This method would also require extremely consistent throwing and trimming throughout the batch.
- Lids have a tendency to be dropped by the user. Factor this risk into the design process. How can you aid the gripping process – does it need to have a knob? Is there a handle in the way that makes it fiddly to grip and lift the lid?
- The weight of the lid is also important. Too light and it can be easy to drop and feel flimsy.
- Other materials, such as wood, which is less breakable, could be considered.
- Is the hole for the lid large enough for the end user to access the interior of the pot to clean it?
- How can the choice of lid impact your piece aesthetically? For example, certain typologies have a more rustic aesthetic and some are more minimal and contemporary.
- Deciding on how to glaze the lid is important. If the lid needs to be fired together with the pot there will need to be an unglazed section so that the two parts won't fuse together during the glaze firing.

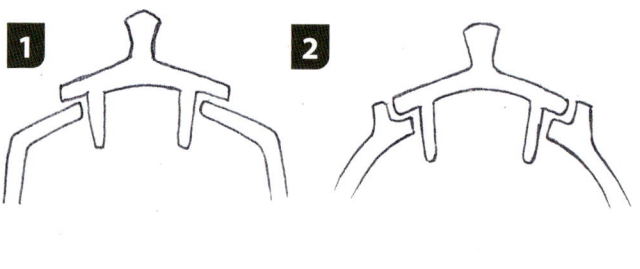
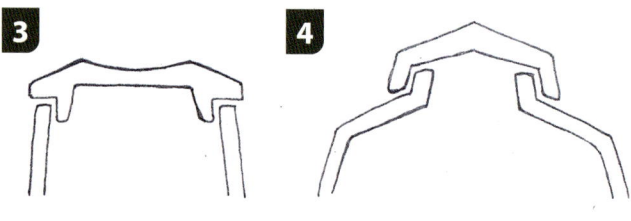
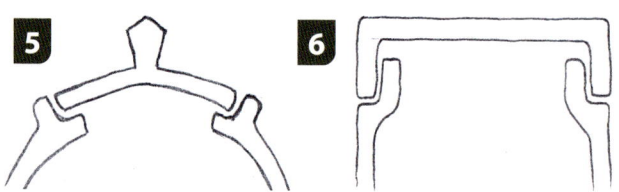

Hand-drawn lid and opening profiles. 1. Demonstrates a lid with a deep flange that holds the lid snugly inside a simple opening 2. Similar but sits inside an opening with a gallery 3. Shows a pot with a simple lip and a lid with a flange, but the lid overhangs the pot very slightly so that the user can more easily grip the lid, as it has no knob 4. Represents a pot with an opening with a raised lip and a lid that sits snugly around the exterior of the lip 5. Has a curved, walled piece with a more simple lid, held only in place by fitting to the flange of the jar 6. Has similarities with profile 4 but the lid is flush to create a more seamless fit.

Often lids are thrown upside down. Here the flange of the lid, which is thrown relatively accurately to fit to the inside of the jar lip, will be trimmed when leather hard to fit the jar and will be turned upside down so that the top of the lid can be finished.

These lids were thrown upside down (as per the previous image) and trimmed to fit each pot exactly. The lid has a very slight overhang to help the user grip the edge of the lid. An angle is trimmed into the shape of the lid. The line of the taper and the concave top of the lid work very nicely with the glaze to create variation and depth. Notice the unglazed lip of the jar so that the pieces can be fired together to reduce warpage and increase the spatial efficiency of the kiln.

A storage jar with a wooden lid made from cherry by Neil Whitelaw. Lids constructed from another material generally need to be made after the firing process to fit the finished piece. Different materials may come with their own problems of warpage or changes as they age. This jar was fired together with a clay 'dummy' lid to help keep its shape in the firing.

An example of a piece with a flush fitting lid, as per 6. in the diagram opposite.

This lid sits on an unglazed raised lip of the teapot and has a deep, snugly fitted flange to hold the lid securely in place when it is in use.

Chapter 2 – Technical Design Considerations

CHAPTER 3

CLAY PREPARATION, THROWING AND TRIMMING PROCESSES

The first practical stages in learning how to make tableware at the wheel include clay preparation, centring clay on the wheel, forming a cylinder and trimming the clay once leather hard. It is also necessary to learn how to reclaim clay to reduce wastage. Once you have mastered these basics, you'll have a solid foundation on which to experiment further. Before beginning with the practical steps, let's familiarise ourselves with our main material: clay.

WHAT IS CLAY?

Many of us will have childhood memories of playing in the garden, digging and finding clay. We likely didn't know what it was called, but perhaps we formed shapes out of it, played with it or heard our gardener parents complaining about it! Clay is a material composed of various minerals and consists of alternating layers of alumina (Al_2), silica ($2SiO_2$) and water $2H_2O$). It is the abundant product of a process of erosion taking place over vast time spans. Sometimes we potters think of a ball of clay as being the beginning of the making process, but indeed, thousands of years have most likely already been spent transforming mineral feldspar from igneous rock (parent material) into clay.

Clay deposits that remain at the site of the parent material are known as primary clays. These clays are often grainy in texture and not very easy to throw with.

Sedimentary is a word to describe clays that have been transported from the site of the parent material by water, ice or wind. These clays are more plastic, finer in particle size and easier to shape. Ball clays and bentonite are good examples of sedimentary clays.

If we were to examine clay under a microscope, it would look a little like a pack of cards, with the cards being almost hexagonal in shape. These cards can slip and slide over each other, without coming unstuck. This quality is essentially what makes clay plastic.

PLASTICITY

We use the word 'plastic' to describe the quality of a material that is soft and can be shaped easily when wet, without reverting back to its original shape. Different clays possess different levels of plasticity.

A good way to test the plasticity of different clays is to take the same quantities and throw the largest and thinnest vessel possible. The one that survives best and doesn't collapse is the most plastic. This tension, or breaking point, is important. It tells us that clay, while being so versatile, is a material with limits. Over time and with much practice, potters can begin to push these limits. In the beginning, however, the best thing to do is to understand and honour these limitations.

A good exercise to help you understand clay and geology is to dig for your own clay. Examine its colour, plasticity and texture. Could you mix in ball clays or grog to improve this? Test its melt to determine firing temperatures. It isn't necessary but you can learn a lot about clay by processing it from the ground yourself.

Pulling the walls of a cylinder.

HOW TO SELECT THE CORRECT CLAY BODY FOR TABLEWARE

We use the term 'clay body' to describe the clay that will form the pot. Bodies can be categorised into types that are usually defined by their range of firing temperatures. We have terracotta, earthenware, stoneware and porcelain.

Terracotta and earthenware are most often, but not exclusively, red in colour when fired. They contain a high amount of iron and their firing temperature is much lower than stoneware and porcelain, approximately 1000°C (1832°F) (cone 06–04). At this temperature, the clay isn't vitrified and isn't as durable as a higher firing body and so it is crucial that the glaze is durable, vitrified and strong. Because it is difficult to achieve such high levels of durability, earthenware bodies would not be my first choice for creating tableware. That is not to say that it can't or shouldn't be done, but it is something to take into consideration when thinking about clay choice.

Stoneware (fired to cone 6+) is a versatile clay, ideal for creating wheel-thrown tableware because it has a high firing temperature, is still very plastic and workable at the wheel, and when fired well is extremely durable. Stoneware is usually grey in colour and can be smooth or grogged but you'll find many options for stoneware in terms of colour, texture and firing range.

Porcelain (fired to cone 8+) is the strongest of the bodies once fired and therefore makes excellent tableware. It is usually (but not always) white in colour, and is very pure and soft, acting as an excellent body for showcasing bright glazes. The main problem with porcelain is that it is a difficult body to throw with and takes a little more time to master. Porcelain can be less plastic and therefore more rigid at the wheel, almost unyielding. For those willing to put in the time, effort and patience, the reward is well worth it.

Many potters experiment with different clays and over time select one or two main bodies to work with. This is partly because of practicalities in that it is logistically difficult to keep swapping between clay bodies without them becoming contaminated and also that different bodies have different firing ranges. When starting out, it is pertinent to think about the tableware you would like to create. If you are inspired by traditional slipware then working with earthenware may be your route; perhaps porcelain really excites you; or maybe you love the earthy and organic qualities of stoneware. The choice is yours, but the body you choose will mean that your glazes and firing schedule will need to be adapted around that.

PREPARATION

Preparing clay is an important and sometimes overlooked part of the making process. Time should be invested in learning techniques such as wedging and kneading clay as well as the weighing out and balling up of clay ready for the wheel.

Preparation can help with the making of tableware in a number of ways. The firmness or softness of the clay is crucial to consider in making different forms. For example, flat forms like plates and low bowls are far quicker and easier to throw using soft (wetter) clay as it is easier to move and manipulate, and as you are not throwing with any height, the strength of the clay is not so important. Slightly firmer (drier) clay is needed for forms like high-sided bowls or cylinders where, if too wet, the weight of the piece will cause it to collapse.

The structure that is created within the clay when wedged and kneaded is also very important in creating a piece of clay that moves with fluidity and strength beneath your hands on the wheel.

Greenware tea bowls thrown in various stoneware clay bodies, some with added grog and others red in colour due to the iron oxide present within the clay body.

Most clay will arrive in 12.5kg (27½lb) bags, pre-mixed and de-aired. In most cases, when making small pieces, using clay cut directly from the bags will be ok, especially if you are not yet confident at kneading. It takes some time to learn how to knead clay without trapping more air pockets than there were before. However, learning how to wedge and knead clay is essential when working with reclaimed clay, if the clay from the manufacturer's bag is too wet/dry or inconsistent, or when creating larger pieces (1kg (2lb) and above). If you are fortunate enough to own a pug mill (*see* Chapter 9) then the good news is that you will not have nearly so much kneading and wedging to do. The pug mill is proficient at removing air.

Wedging

Wedging is the process of homogenising the consistency of the clay, removing the majority of the air pockets and getting the clay ready to work with. Generally, clay that is taken straight from the manufacturer's bag does not need to be wedged, but if you are reclaiming clay or using a more inconsistent, perhaps foraged clay, wedging is really important. Wedging can also be used to combine two or more clay bodies together to create a new clay blend.

The process of wedging is a repetitive activity that follows a simple and laborious routine. The clay is cut in half (or if combining two clay bodies, the two bodies are pressed together) and then the top and bottom layers are rotated,

In this example, we're combining two different clay bodies together, but the process is the same for all wedging. Two pieces of clay the same size and shape are pressed together and cut through horizontally with a wire.

Both pieces of clay are then rotated 90 degrees. One piece is left on the workbench and the other piece is then lifted above your head, then dropped back onto the clay on the workbench, letting the weight of the clay and gravity do the work. You now have four layers of clay.

Cut through the clay again and repeat the process. This piece is a cut-through of the previous iteration demonstrating four layers of clay.

This cut-through demonstrates eight layers of clay. Here we are rotating the bottom piece of clay before the next drop.

This is a cut-through demonstrating sixteen layers.

A cut-through again at a later iteration; you can see the clay is beginning to blend.

Lifting the top layer and rotating ready for the next drop, using gravity over strength to remove the air pockets.

The clay is now almost blended on its eighth iteration, but you can keep going until the clay is fully blended.

The clay is now fully blended with no lines (if using two different clays) or air pockets visible and is ready to be kneaded before being used for throwing.

creating layer upon layer. The top piece is then lifted high (above your head) and dropped down again with force onto the bottom piece of clay that is resting on the table. You are using the weight of the clay to remove air pockets and blend the clays together. This process of cutting, rotating, lifting and dropping down is repeated until the two clays are fully blended. With each repetition the number of layers in the clay is doubled, leading to the clay becoming thoroughly blended and wedged.

Kneading

There are two general techniques for kneading: ram's head and spiral. Both do the same thing and which to use is really a personal preference. The spiral technique is my preference. It takes longer to master than the ram's head technique but I find it to be more effective and less tiring when working with a larger amount of clay.

The main objectives when kneading clay are to remove any air pockets from the clay body and to align the clay platelets in layers, which makes it easier to throw with. A pocket of air in a piece of clay that is being thrown de-centres the clay, making the area around the air pocket uneven. When throwing at the wheel, you can remove the air pocket using a needle tool but this does not always work, and even when it does remove the air, the clay can be left marked and uneven. If a pocket of air remains in the clay throughout the firing process, there is a risk of the pot exploding in the kiln as the air expands within the clay and searches for a way out.

You can choose to knead a large piece of clay from which you will cut smaller pieces to throw with, or knead a piece of clay weighed out to make a single piece, for example if you were throwing a large vase.

Clay is kneaded by being rocked back and forth in the hands against the surface of a work table, with pressure being applied on the downward motion. As the clay is rocked back up, your hands can change position slightly, ready for the next downward push. The downward force helps to burst small pockets of air while winding the clay up in a spiral structure. Although both methods require a certain amount of force in order to be successful, time should be spent practising technique so that there is as little impact on your body as possible. Rather than using force from your wrists, arms and back, try to adopt a rocking motion with your entire body. The height of the work table is also very important in reducing the impact on your body; it should be ideally around hip height. If you are constructing your own work table, it is worthwhile testing out a few different heights before a final design is decided.

Ram's Head Technique

The hands work together to rock the clay back towards the body.

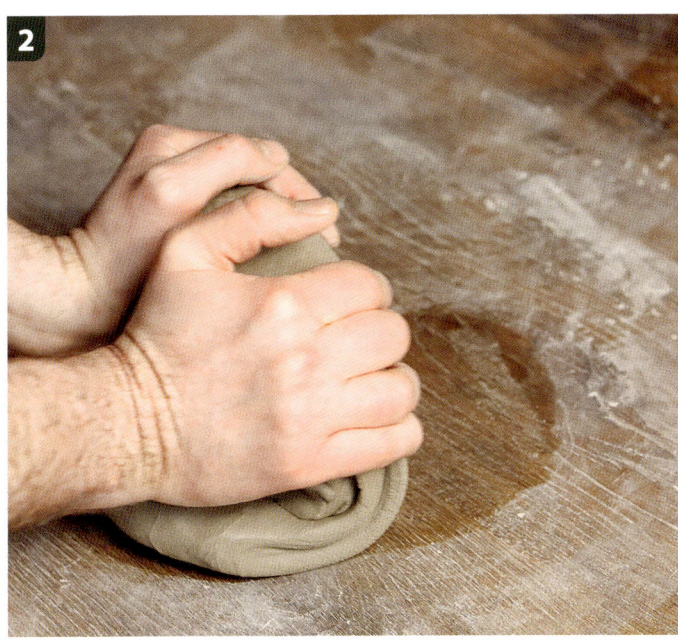

Adjust your grip so that the heels of both hands are positioned to apply even pressure.

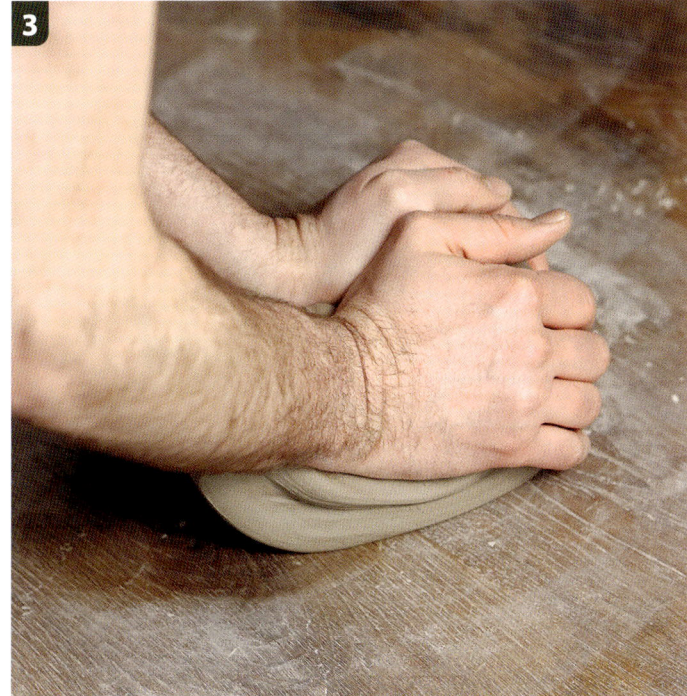

Rock your body forwards, applying pressure with both arms to compress the clay onto the workbench. The hands work together to push the clay down and also to prevent the clay from being spread sideways.

As a rule of thumb, this motion should be repeated at least 100 times to create an effectively kneaded piece of clay. You can see a spiral created and it looks a little bit like a ram's head!

Spiral Technique

The spiral method follows much of the same principles as the ram's head; however, instead of the hands being used with equal force to push the clay down and inwards, attention is paid to the 'heart' of the spiral, which is not moved in a straightforward up/down motion. A twist is created when slightly changing the position of your hands on the upward motion and pushing down to one side and rocking back centrally.

The first step of working with an irregular piece of clay is to start rocking it back and forth on a tabletop. The clay should soon form a curved underside.

Next, to create the spiral, imagine there is a clock face on your table with the clay in the centre; rock the clay forward to the 11-o'clock position. Use the heel of your right hand to apply the pressure whilst the left hand helps support and guide the motion.

Then move the clay to the 12-o'clock position and rock back towards your body. During the rocking of the clay back towards yourself, adjust the placement of your hands – you should notice that they have twisted around slightly.

Remove your hands from the clay and put them back in their original position.

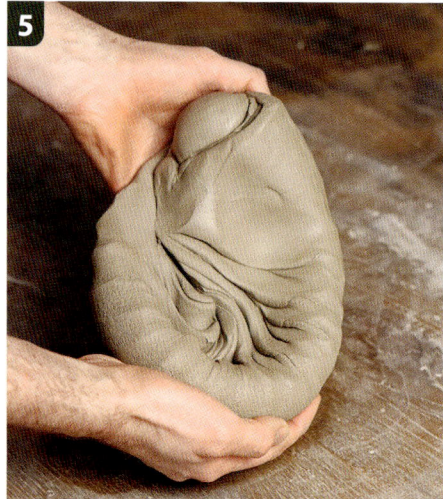

With practice, this should become one fluid movement so that, with repetition, the rocking and winding of the clay will create a spiral structure. The heart of the spiral should always be a comfortable amount of clay to grasp between your hands, about the size of a fist.

To wind the clay back up into a piece to be thrown with or divided into smaller pieces, start to grasp a slightly larger amount of clay each time you reposition your hands and apply less force when rocking the clay downwards.

WEIGHING AND PREPARING TO THROW

Once the clay is wedged and kneaded, a pot can be thrown with it (although unless the clay is already the correct weight, it will need to be weighed out to the desired amount). Pat firmly with your hands into a neat and rounded ball (the more perfect the shape at this point, the easier the centring will be). If you need to combine two or more pieces of clay to meet your desired weight, be careful not to trap air in the join. I often place the smaller piece of clay on the tabletop and carefully throw down the larger piece on top – the force helps to push any potential air out.

THROWING TOOLS IN MORE DETAIL

Sponge
A sponge is essential. It is used to add and remove water when throwing a pot. A sponge can also be used as an extension of your hand, and may be used to help pull the walls of a pot smoothly by being positioned between the outer wall of the pot and your knuckle or fingertips. It can also be used in a similar way when compressing or finishing the lip of a pot, or when shaping the inside surface. Due to the softly textured surface, a sponge will leave marks behind when used, which may require cleaning up and finishing with a rib tool.

A sponge on a stick is required to remove excess water from inside a closed form, such as a bottle, jug or narrow mug that the potter's hand can't reach inside without damaging.

Potter's Needle
A potter's needle is a very simple yet versatile tool. Among many other things, it can be used to check the thickness of a pot's base, to pierce any unwanted bubbles of trapped air in the clay or even as a fine blade to cut away an uneven rim.

Rib Tool
Ribs come in a variety of shapes, sizes and materials. They are often also referred to as kidneys due to their common rounded kidney shape. When throwing, I generally like to have next to me three ribs, each made from a different material: a wooden rib, flexible stainless steel rib and rubber rib. The choice of rib changes depending on the shape and size of the pot and the stage in the throwing process it is being used in. The general use of a rib is to help form, shape and refine the pot.

A wooden rib is useful as an aid for moving clay. The inflexibility of the material means that it can be used to move clay when pulling up the walls of a pot, for example. I tend to use a wooden rib on larger pots.

A stainless steel rib offers a balance between rigidity and flexibility. They are stamped out of thin sheet metal, giving them a sharp edge. This can be used as a trimming tool, but when working with wet clay can easily cut into the surface. I generally use this type of rib as a finishing tool to define the shape of a pot and create a smooth surface.

Rubber/silicone ribs are available in a variety of hardness; the more clay we are attempting to move, the harder the rib we choose. A long, slightly curved, firm rib is useful when forming the surface of a plate. A curved medium-hard rib is useful for forming the inside of bowls. A small, soft kidney-shaped rib is great as an all-rounder, especially for finishing the surface of a pot.

Chamois Leather
A wet strip of chamois leather can be gently held between finger and thumb then placed over the lip of a nearly finished pot to remove excess slip, compress and (with careful pressure from the fingers holding it) add definition.

Solid Metal Turning Tool
A square metal trimming tool is used to remove excess clay from the base of a pot. It is held flat to the wheel head and pressed into the base of a spinning pot until most of the excess clay is removed.

The pointed metal trimming tool is used in a similar way to the square metal trimming tool; this tool is used to create a small undercut at the base of a pot for the wire to be guided into.

Potter's Wire
To remove a pot from the wheel, a wire, typically a fine, flexible, twisted wire with handles on either end, is held taut between two hands and dragged along the surface of the wheel underneath the pot (guided by the undercut in the pot's base). This allows the pot to then be lifted from the wheel.

Typical tools for use when throwing at the wheel. Which tools you should use is quite a personal choice, but these are my most-used items.

Throwing Gauge
A throwing gauge is a useful piece of equipment for repetition throwing. It can be set to the specific measurements you need to throw to and is usually set to the measurement of a pot lip. Arms can be added to the gauge to measure other aspects, such as the belly of a jug.

CENTRING

Centring is perhaps the most fundamental aspect of the throwing process. Think of this as being the groundwork that will determine the success of your finished pot. If the clay is not centred properly, it will skew off to one side and then problems will occur later in the wall thicknesses and it will be generally unbalanced.

Centring is the process of applying pressure to the clay as the wheel spins until it is aligned in the centre of the wheel. We are using the motion of the wheel to align the particles of the clay into a spiral shape. It is this spiral shape

Prepare the throwing surface – wheel head or bat – by removing any dust or dry clay residue with a damp sponge. Make sure the surface isn't too wet as it will be difficult to get the clay ball to adhere. Slowly spin the wheel and apply a damp sponge to its surface. If you are throwing multiple pieces that you are wiring and lifting off the wheel then there will be a thin pad of clay left behind – you don't need to clean this away or dampen it between pots.

Firmly place the ball of clay onto the centre of the wheel. Allow the wheel to slowly spin and pat the clay down repeatedly and evenly to compress and attach to the centre of the wheel.

Next, slip your hands into a bowl of water or use a sponge to wet the ball of clay. Speed your wheel right up. With both elbows securely anchored to your body, place your right hand around the clay, ready to pull towards the centre of the wheel, and your left hand ready to push forwards into the centre of the wheel.

Bringing the clay back down is the next process. Whilst the wheel is spinning, push the clay down and slightly forwards with the heel of the thumb of your right hand, and with your hands linked together, your left hand takes over and pushes down whilst your right hand supports the outside of the clay. If you feel the clay sticking to your hands and dragging, add more water. The process of coning up and pushing the clay back down can be repeated until the clay is centred.

Once the clay is centred, press down with your left hand firmly, still using the right hand to contain the outside so that you can control the diameter of the disc of clay. Think about the pot you are about to make and compress the clay to the desired diameter to begin forming your piece from.

If you have successfully centred your clay then with the wheel spinning it should look and feel absolutely regular.

that gives the centred clay its strength. By moving the clay up into a tall cone and then pressing it back down into a flattened cylinder, usually two or three times, the clay will become centred and compressed. It's important to master centring before moving on to the next stages.

CYLINDERS

The next steps follow on from the process of centring and will enable you to form a cylinder. The cylindrical shape is the basis of many forms and so perfecting this shape is important and time well spent.

Tips and Troubleshooting

It is a good idea to position a mirror in front of yourself, angled to give you a view of a pot's profile. This will stop the need for you to bend awkwardly to see your pot side-on, and can be used between or during pulls to check your work.

Decide how thick you need the base to be; does your design have a flat base or a foot-ring? To check this, you can

With the wheel spinning, steady both hands together and, using a finger from your dominant hand, find the centre of the clay. If you apply just a very small amount of pressure, rather than the motion of the wheel taking your finger around, you should feel it drawn downwards.

With your hands still linked together, push down with your fingertip into the centre of the clay until you have reached the required depth. Use one finger to make contact with the clay whilst a finger from your other hand sits on top to help stabilise and push downwards.

To open up the pot, create a hook with the finger of your dominant hand, and using the finger of your other hand to support it, apply steady pressure. Pull the clay towards your body, keeping your fingers parallel and at a consistent height from the wheel until the pot has been opened up to the desired measurement. You can support the outside of the pot if you wish but be careful not to squeeze the clay as this will prematurely pull up the walls.

Use a sponge to rid the base of any excess water or slurry and use either your finger, or the sponge underneath your fingertip, to firmly work backwards and forwards from the centre of the base to the bottom right (or five-o'clock position). This not only tidies the base, it also compresses it, which will prevent cracks appearing in the drying or firing stages. Be careful not to press too hard as you don't want to thin the base.

From this point onwards, your hands should remain in the same position on the wheel. From your point of view, keep your right hand on the outside of the pot and your left hand on the inside of the pot, both at the 5-o'clock position. When learning, it is easy to allow your hands to move with the direction of the wheel, but remember that the wheel should be doing all the work and your fingers are guiding the clay.

You are now ready to begin moving the clay upwards in a series of pulls to create the walls of the pot. The first pull only needs to guide the walls of the clay into a cone shape. Position your right-hand knuckle at the base on the outside of the pot, with your left-hand finger placed inside the pot at the base of the wall, and move your hands upwards as one.

Once your hands have reached the top of the pot, you will need to set the lip of the pot. Place the index finger and thumb of your left hand either side of the lip and with the index finger of your right hand gently press down with even pressure. This will remove excess slip from the pot as well as help keep the rim of the pot level. After each pull, the lip of the pot should be set.

These next few pulls will focus on moving clay upwards into a cylindrical wall of even thickness. With each pull, position your hands as before, with the right-hand knuckle or fingertip outside the pot at its base, and the left-hand fingertip resting inside the pot at the base of the wall. With your fingers in this position, push the knuckle of your right hand slightly into the pot and then the left-hand finger into the wall of the pot. You should see a bulge of clay, pushed out by the inside finger above the outside knuckle.

With your hands now set in position, move upwards and inwards as a unit, bringing with you the bulge of clay. As you bring your hands up, be careful not to squeeze them together as this will result in uneven walls that are thick at the base and get thinner towards the top. Repeat this whole process until the desired height has been reached; with practice, this should take two or three pulls. Remember, during each pull it is important to maintain a constant wheel speed, constant hand speed and even pressure between your two hands.

Your fingers throughout this process must remain staggered in height, with your outside knuckle lower than your inside finger – they are naturally set apart by the thickness of clay in the base of the pot. Connect your two hands together with your thumbs so they move together as one.

The centrifugal force of the wheel is always pushing the clay outwards, so until the desired height of the pot is reached, a cylinder should be kept slightly conical. As your hands reach the rim of the pot, gently release pressure and remove your hands.

Once the walls have been pulled up to reach the desired height, it is time to finish the shape of your cylinder. If you wish to have curved walls then you will need to pull the clay slightly higher than the finished measurements, as when you push the clay out from the inside the height will reduce. If you are pushing the rim of the pot outwards to a specific point then make sure that it is thicker to start with as it will thin out the wider it is stretched.

13 Up until this point, the only tools used have been your hands and perhaps a sponge. Before finishing the wall of the pot, excess clay can be removed from the base of the pot by holding a square-edged trimming tool to the wheel head, carefully pushing into the base of the pot as the wheel turns.

14 A rib tool can now be used to smooth and compress the walls of the pot. The rib is held against the outside wall of the pot and moved from bottom to top, with your left hand inside the pot supporting the inner wall. When using a rib tool, be careful to hold it at a slight angle away from yourself. If you hold a rib tool vertically against a spinning pot it can create a jittering effect on the clay and may even snag on and buckle your pot. Whenever tools are used, try to think of them as an extension of your hands.

15 Excess water must now be removed with a sponge from inside the pot. If you cannot reach inside the pot without damaging it then a sponge on a stick can be used.

16 There are various things to consider when finishing the rim of a pot, but as a general rule it should be compressed one final time, any slip should be removed and it should be given its final shape by using your fingers, a sponge or a piece of chamois leather.

17 Before wiring off from the wheel, an undercut needs to be made using a pointed trimming tool. This tool should be held flat against the wheel head as it turns and pressed into the base of the pot to create a small groove that will guide the wire when cutting the pot away from the wheel.

18 To remove a pot from the wheel, hold a potter's wire taut between your hands and drag along the wheel head, through the grooves you have just made and underneath the pot.

19 Making sure both your hands and pot are dry, place your hands around the pot, being careful not to cause distortion. Gently lift the pot from the wheel and carefully place it on a ware board. The wheel can also be turned slightly to help the release. If your pot feels stuck then repeat the wiring-off process.

stop the wheel and push a needle tool vertically down until it touches the wheel head; use your finger to mark on the needle where the base of your pot is and, with your finger in place, pull the needle back out – the measurement between the tip of the needle tool and your finger will give you an idea of the thickness of clay in the base.

To ensure that the walls of the cylinder are of even thickness, the speed of both the wheel and your hands moving up the pot must be consistent throughout each pull. If, for example, your hand speed slows down then this will cause the wall of the pot to become thinner.

When pulling up the clay, link your two hands in some way so instead of working independently from one another they work as a unit. Combined with the motion of the spinning wheel, this hand position forces the clay upwards between the inside and outside hands.

If the pot starts to open out too much at the top, it can be collared back in to maintain the tapered shape. This can be done between pulls. With the wheel spinning at a steady speed, use both hands to apply even pressure around the entire pot at the point it has flared out. Be careful not to apply too much or uneven pressure otherwise the pot can buckle and fall in on itself. Once you have collared the pot in, reset the rim (as you would between pulls), as the collaring can easily create a wobble in the rim.

If you notice an excess amount of clay at the base of your pot, make sure to focus on moving it upwards. Apply pressure from your right-hand finger to the outside base of the pot, feel the excess clay push above the finger and then proceed with pulling this clay up. If you are doing this after a pull or two, be careful not to squeeze the walls thinner as your hands travel up the pot; it may be that you are barely touching the clay as your hands rise, with all the work happening lower down.

You can throw directly onto the wheel head or a bat/bat system. Bats are usually used for large pots, or pots that are likely to distort when taken off the wheel by hand, such as open bowls or plates. The pot is then removed later when firm enough to handle; it might need to be wired off for a second time.

DRYING WARES

It is important to understand how clay behaves in your studio and how it is affected by the environment and climate around it. The goal is to dry pots in a controlled and consistent way. Ideally, the drying process should be away from direct sunlight, fluctuations of heat and dramatic changes in humidity; however, this is not often possible, especially for a potter with a small studio that has a kiln in the same room as any drying pots. Our studio, for example, is a single room so we control the environment of drying pots by placing ware boards in trolleys and covering them with plastic sheets.

Wares need to be carefully dried to a leather-hard consistency before they can be trimmed and have other components, such as handles, attached.

We often use plastic sheets to cover wares in our studio. If it is very hot, spritz water underneath the sheet and seal tightly.

If making plates then they may be left completely uncovered for a day, wired off and removed from their throwing bats, and then covered in plastic sheets for a further day or two to create a climate where all the plates are the same consistency.

Other forms, such as mugs, are covered loosely with plastic overnight so there is a little airflow. Make sure there is no plastic sheeting touching the clay. The following day the mugs are carefully dried until the consistency is right for trimming and attaching handles. This process is a good example of how a seemingly simple everyday form such as a mug can be tricky to make. If the mug body dries too quickly then the rim can become nearly bone dry while the bottom part of the mug is still too wet to trim, and an attempt at attaching a handle to the inconsistent clay will most likely result in a crack forming at the handle joint and an unsafe handle. To allow pots to be evenly dried they can also be turned upside down and rested on their rim to allow the underside to dry.

TRIMMING

There are many ways a pot can be transformed by being trimmed, from simply neatening the base of a pot to creating a decorative foot-ring.

A pot is ready to trim when it is no longer wet or sticky to touch and is able to hold its shape when held without distorting. If a pot is left to dry for too long then it can make trimming difficult, especially if it reaches the bone-dry stage. Avoid trimming bone-dry work as it creates harmful dust that should not be breathed in or allowed to rest in the fabric of your clothing. If you must trim this type of work, wear a suitable face mask fitted with a fine-particle filter (of P3/P100 grade) and dampen the pot with a sponge or spray to reduce dust.

By contrast, a pot that is still too wet at the trimming stage will be prone to distortion and collapse. It's important to take time to learn your clay and environment in order to control the drying process. A useful piece of studio furniture is a damp cupboard, a cabinet that can hold ware boards in which the airflow can be controlled. A damp cupboard can be replicated by simply covering pots with plastic sheeting.

To trim a pot, it must first be turned upside down, centred and secured to the wheel head. The simplest method of doing this is to place the pot upside down, slowly spinning the wheel and gradually moving the pot until it is centred, before securing it to the wheel using three evenly spaced pieces of clay pressed firmly. Alternatively, a pot can be placed on a wheel that has been slightly dampened with a sponge. Push the pot forwards and backwards gently and

Trimming is the process of turning away excess clay from the underside of a leather-hard pot to create the finished form (this process can also be called turning).

Many forms, such as bowls, require excess clay to be left at the base during throwing to help support the weight of wet clay. But once this has partly dried out and the pot can support itself and hold its shape, then trimming can be commenced.

the water will hold the pot in place without the need for additional pieces of clay.

Centring a Pot for Trimming

Many wheels are marked with concentric circles that can help in positioning a pot centrally, although adjustments may still need to be made. Hold a needle tool steadily in two hands at a point on the pot wall close to the base of the upturned pot. Start the wheel spinning without the tool touching the pot and very gradually move the needle tool closer. Eventually the tool will scrape on the spinning pot. At this point, hold still and let the pot turn a couple more complete circles with the needle tool making a slight scratch into the side. Now spin the wheel so that the centre point of the mark you have just made in the pot is positioned towards the centre of your body and stop the wheel with the pot in this position. With two hands, push the pot gently away from your body and repeat this whole process until the mark left by the needle is consistent around the pot. With practice you will be able to do this process by eye, without the need for a needle tool.

Chamois Leather

As an alternative to using three pieces of clay to secure a pot to the wheel, a chamois leather can be used. Simply soak a chamois leather in water and wring the water out; then lay the chamois over the wheel and place the upturned pot directly onto the chamois – there is no need to secure the pot in place with three pieces of clay. There are two main benefits in using this method. When trimming a number of pots, this can help speed up the process as all you need to do is centre the pot and the chamois leather will hold the pot in place. The chamois leather reduces the risk of indentations being made in the pot by the clay securing it to the wheel, which is particularly common when attempting to trim a pot that is still a little too wet. The down sides are that if the chamois is too wet or becomes too dry then the pot may slide away, and also the rim of the pot may slightly flatten onto the chamois leather, requiring fettling to repair the rim.

Chucks

Chucks are an extremely useful aid for trimming, especially for trimming forms that are not able to balance on their rim on the wheel, such as a bottle, and for pots that have an uneven or delicate rim, such as a jug with a spout. A chuck is also a means of speeding up the trimming and centring process.

A chuck works best when leather hard and at the same consistency as the pots that are being held on it and trimmed. I usually throw the chuck on a throwing bat at the end of the batch of pots that will be later trimmed on it. The shape of a chuck will vary depending on the form that is needing to be trimmed. I use three general chuck forms that can be adapted for different uses.

Using a piece of chamois leather to trim directly onto, keeping the ware in place without needing to secure it with clay.

A 'cone' chuck, ideal for using to trim cylinders.

A 'cooling tower' chuck, ideal for using to place ware inside to trim.

A 'doughnut' chuck, ideal for using to trim items such as lids.

TRIMMING TOOLS IN MORE DETAIL

Ribbon Tool
A ribbon tool is made from bevelled strips of hooped steel attached to a wooden handle. The shape of the metal hoop can vary in size for different functions. Large, gently curved hoops are suitable for removing large portions of clay smoothly and rapidly. Small, thin, pointed hoops are used for precise and delicate trimming.

Solid Metal Turning Tool
This tool is made from a flat piece of metal with a folded end that can be shaped in many different ways (square, pointed, rounded). The end of the tool is sharpened with bevelled edges, which when pressed at roughly 90 degrees against a spinning pot, shave ribbons of clay away.

Steel Rib
I often use a flexible stainless steel rib (both a kidney-shaped one and a rectangular one) for finishing the surface of the pot. The sharp edges can be used as a trimming tool themselves when held at roughly 90 degrees to the pot, and can be used to remove small amounts of clay and create a regular surface on the face of a pot. If held at a sharper angle to the face of the pot, the tool will smooth the surface of the pot. Be careful not to cut yourself on this tool (especially when using your fingers to clean clay from its surface) as, through use, the clay can sharpen the steel, resulting in a razor-sharp edge.

Rubber/Silicone Rib
Silicone ribs can be used in a similar way to a steel rib except they only smooth the clay. They can be used to soften marks and sharp edges left behind from throwing and trimming.

Needle Tool
The needle tool is used to mark reference points while trimming a pot.

Callipers
Callipers set to specific measurements can be used to speed up the marking out a foot-ring on a pot.

Trimming Spinner
A trimming spinner is used to hold a pot in place when being trimmed (an upturned jam jar lid works well for this purpose).

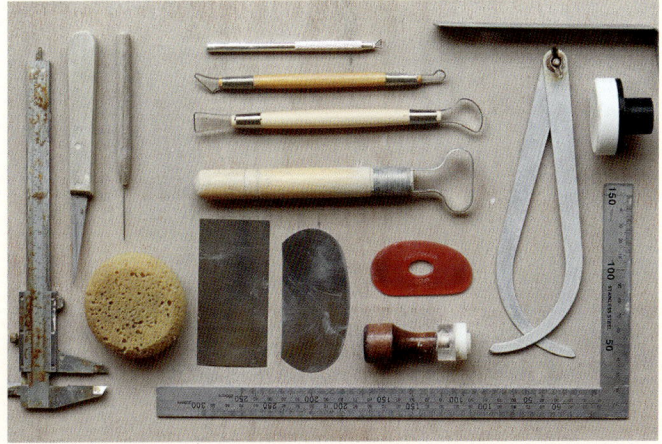
Some of the main tools used for the trimming process, including a ruler, callipers, ribbon tools, a sponge, a pin tool and a knife.

Chapter 3 – Clay Preparation, Throwing and Trimming Processes

Tips and Troubleshooting

When trimming a pot, you can use a finger, rested and applying a little pressure on the centre of the base of your pot, to help keep it in place and act as an anchor to keep your hands and tool steady.

If the base of your pot is particularly thin or the clay is too wet then it is likely to become misshapen when being held in place. Also, if trimming many pots, the friction of the clay spinning against your finger can become uncomfortable. You can use a 'trimming spinner'. Place your finger on the top part, which remains motionless, while the bottom part is in contact with the pot and spins with it, alleviating any friction on your finger and minimising any damage to the base of your pot.

As with throwing, it is useful to create a solid structure by connecting your hands and body. Where possible, try to keep your hands connected so they work together as a unit rather than independently. I hold the trimming tool in my right hand with it steadied by the thumb of my left hand, while the index finger of my left hand is touching the centre of the pot.

Use the ribbon tool to remove clay from the walls of your cylinder or form. This could be to remove any unwanted throwing rings or marks, or to further define the shape. Start at the corner-point of the base, moving down towards the wheel head for as far as you intend to trim.

To gauge the thickness of the walls while trimming, you can tap the pot at different points; as the sound of the taps varies this will tell you how the thickness of the walls varies too. A dull and low-pitched sound means the walls are thick, whereas a higher-pitched sound means the walls are thinner. Practice and experience will help you to recognise these sounds. Alternatively, you can remove the pot from the wheel and inspect the pot by feel and sight, but this means that it will have to be re-centred on before you continue to trim.

If you are removing a lot of clay, pay attention to the thickness of the walls of the pot. It is easy to trim too much or too little, which can result in a pot being unbalanced, or in the worst case, to trim the wall so thinly that the pot collapses or a hole is trimmed out.

Some forms are more difficult to grip than others when removing from the wheel, such as plates and flat bowls. We would recommend trimming these on a bat that is attached to the wheel with wheel pins – the clay bat could also have a chamois leather or clay chuck on. Instead of using your hands to remove the trimmed pot, you can remove the clay bat entirely, then place another bat on your pot (sandwiching it between the two). Applying enough pressure to prevent the bats and pot from slipping, yet without distorting the pot, flip the bats over (like flipping a cake out of its tin by using cooling racks). Carefully remove what is now the top bat from the lip of the pot.

Neatening Up

Once centred, trim the flat underside of the pot so that it is level and any wire marks are removed. If the base is left uneven at this point, the uneven shape is likely to remain and be exaggerated as you continue to trim.

Trim away any uneven clay from the side of the pot.

If working to measurements, measure and mark the foot-ring or base diameter of the pot. Callipers and a needle are useful tools for this, though a ruler and needle tool can work just as well. When marking out, the needle needs to be held steady to the pot for at least one full rotation of the wheel. The first stage of trimming is now complete, and the pot should appear even and regular when spinning on the wheel.

Trimming Pots without a Foot-Ring

Use the ribbon tool to finish the base of your pot. Although there is no foot-ring, you will need to ensure that the pot sits on a defined point (which behaves like a foot-ring). If you trim a base absolutely flat, you are not guaranteed that the base will remain flat through the drying and firing processes, which will create an unstable and wobbly pot. To create this defined point on which your pot will sit, you must trim the base so that it is (at least slightly) concave. Use the ribbon tool, running it from the centre of the pot outwards.

A bevel can also be trimmed into the base of the pot at its edge. This performs three functions: it further defines the point on which the pot sits, making it more stable; it lifts the form, giving it the appearance of being lighter in weight; and it creates a point to where glaze can be applied that is raised from the ground, meaning that during the glaze firing there is less risk of the pot fusing to the kiln shelf.

Trimming Pots with a Foot-Ring

For this example, I am using a bowl, but foot-rings can be trimmed into a variety of forms. Work on the clay outside the foot-ring. Use the ribbon tool to remove excess clay as required. You may want to produce a smooth, continuous curve from the lip to the foot of the pot, or divide the form in a more angular way, creating walls and an underside.

With a pointed ribbon tool, cut away a groove inside of the foot-ring that you marked earlier. This groove can be nearly as deep as the finished foot-ring and will act as a reference point as well as protective stopper, so that you don't unintentionally cut away the foot-ring.

Carefully trim away excess clay from the centre of the base. To maintain balance, try to mirror the inside shape of the pot.

Trim the profile of the foot-ring as desired; it can be tall, short, angular, rounded and so on. I generally trim a bevel into the foot, so that there is a fine point upon which the pot will make contact with the surface it is sitting on.

A steel rib, held at an angle relatively flat to the pot, can be used to clean up the markings made by the trimming tool on the base and walls. Alternatively, a silicone rib can be used to perform a similar job, but rather than removing markings left by tools or hands it softens them. Finally, any sharp edges can be softened by your fingertips or a silicone rib.

You may choose to give the foot-ring an undercut. This will act as a channel for glaze to sit in, or if a glaze has a lot of movement, to collect in rather than run onto the kiln shelf. It also creates a clean and easy edge that wax can be applied to and glaze wiped away from. Either a pointed metal trimming tool or a small, fine ribbon tool can be used to create the undercut. If you are glazing the base inside the foot-ring then another undercut can be made on the inside face.

Finishing and Removing from the Wheel

With firm and even pressure, press the stamp of your maker's mark into the finished pot, being careful not to distort its shape.

It's important to take care when removing a trimmed pot from the wheel, especially if it has been secured firmly to the wheel or chuck. It is all too easy to distort or even crack a pot at this stage. Place both hands around the pot, covering the surface and applying a light grip as evenly as possible. Start to lift the pot directly upwards; if the pot seems stuck down firmly and isn't coming away, then whilst still gripping the pot with your hands, start to turn the wheel at a very slow speed.

Using a damp sponge, fettle the lip of the pot to remove any marks left behind from where the pot has been attached to the wheel.

Embossing a Maker's Mark

Once the pot is trimmed, a maker's mark can be pressed into the clay. If pressing the maker's mark into the centre of the base of a pot, which might be liable to distortion or cracking when pressure from the stamp is applied, use a tool or chuck to support the inside face of the pot when pressure is applied. If you know a form is likely to be damaged when stamped, you can make a chuck, at the same time as the pot, that is designed to support the inside base.

The place least likely to distort or crack when the maker's mark is applied is at the edge of the foot, either on the underside or wall of the pot. The positioning of your maker's mark will depend on your preferred aesthetic, as well as how it will practically be affected by glaze or potential damage it might cause to the pot.

We are using a laser-cut stamp to mark our work here, but maker's marks can be carved out of clay, painted on with oxide, added using a decal and so on. The are many options available.

In this instance, one of our maker's mark options is used on the underside of a mug form, which will not be glazed. The clay is supported inside the pot by a chuck, preventing distortion.

This is a smaller and more discrete maker's mark embossed into the bevelled edge beneath the handle join.

RECLAIMING CLAY

This is the process of returning excess clay from the throwing or trimming processes – too wet or dry – back into a usable state. Any clay that has not been fired is able to be reclaimed and reused and so this is an essential process to master as part of your studio production, reducing waste and preserving precious resources. If time is not a problem, all of these types of clay (trimmings, too wet, too dry) can be reclaimed in the same way, in the same bucket. A bucket with a lid is ideal to prevent any other materials entering the reclaim.

Add any clay that you need to reclaim in the bucket and make sure it is fully saturated with water. If, for example, a reclaim bucket is filled with clay trimmings, top up with water so that all the clay is below the surface. Let the clay slake for a week or more to ensure that all leather-hard clay is re-saturated, then remove any excess clear water that is sitting on the surface with a sponge, being careful not to disturb the clay below. To reduce the risk of creating clay dust, immediately put clay trimmings into a bucket of water or slip rather than allowing them to dry out first – this means that the clay will need to be slaked for longer in the bucket, as leather-hard clay rehydrates much slower than bone-dry clay.

Place the reclaim onto a dry plaster bat (*see* Chapter 9 for how to make your own). Depending on the consistency you can use your hands or a vessel to move the clay. The plaster bat absorbs the excess water from the clay. When the clay is at the desired consistency, it can then be wedged (or pug milled) and kneaded in preparation for the wheel.

A simple plaster bat can be made; however, there are alternatives, such as using an unvarnished wooden board or work surface, or even by filling an old pillowcase with reclaim and stringing it up to dry.

CHAPTER 4

STEP-BY-STEP MAKING PROCESSES

This chapter consists of practical technical advice, plus some troubleshooting tips, in a series of step-by-step guides. Please see the previous chapters for more detailed analysis on the design considerations for each form.

USING WOODEN BATS

Attaching a wooden bat to the wheel head is invaluable when making wheel-thrown plates and bowls. It is extremely difficult to remove a plate from the wheel without a bat, as the plate, having such a wide surface area, is prone to distortion. If the plate has a flat rim, it would most likely collapse. Instead of removing the thrown clay, you remove the bat itself from the wheel head and then start again with a fresh bat for your next piece.

Using a bat will also enable you to make a piece that is larger in diameter than the wheel head, which is useful if you're working on a platter form.

The downsides of using throwing bats held to the wheel with clay pads is that the pads are not always 100 per cent successful at holding the bat in place, especially if you use the piece of clay for a number of times. Furthermore, if you are using a throwing gauge to measure the piece, the height may slowly decrease with each new bat/ware insertion, as the clay pad is being repeatedly compressed. This means that the throwing gauge needs to be checked and adjusted each time a new bat is used.

In order to attach the bat to the wheel head, first throw a flat disc of clay directly onto the wheel; then use your fingers to make circular ring impressions as well as straight cross-section lines into the clay. These grooves will help the wooden bat remain in place with no movement when the wheel is spinning.

Place the bat onto the clay disc, move the bat forwards and backwards slightly, and press down firmly. A plate can now be thrown onto the bat.

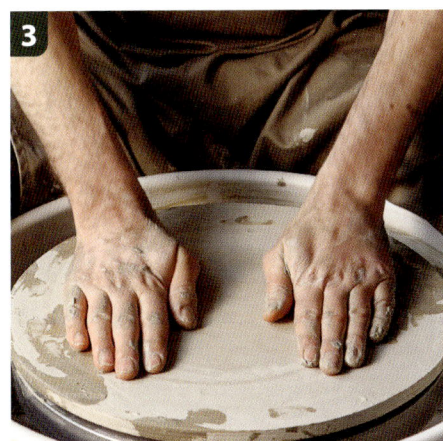

To remove the bat, use a tool to carefully prise away the bat from the clay. The next bat can be attached to this same pad of clay, and so on.

Attaching a pulled handle to a mug body.

Alternatively, you can install wheel pins on your wheel head, and drill corresponding holes in each bat so that it can be slotted onto the wheel. Some wheel manufacturers make wheel heads that bats can fit inside. It is also possible to make your own bats. We have used plywood cut into circles, though various bat systems are available from pottery suppliers.

PLATES

Tips for Throwing Plates

Preparing your clay is important. Clay that is relatively soft is usually preferable, though this can also make the plate more vulnerable to warping and slumping when removing from the wheel, especially if that plate has a rim. Using reclaimed

Centre the clay as usual. Once centring is achieved, carefully compress the clay to the wheel head, making sure that your hands control the movement of the clay as it spreads out across the wheel. If you attempt to move the clay too quickly and/or without enough resistance from your outside hand, then as the disc widens it will become irregular in shape.

Be careful to evenly distribute the clay as you widen the disc. With each compression, apply even pressure, bringing out the clay to its required width; then compress one last time with a rib tool. It is important to make sure the clay is thoroughly and evenly compressed as this will help prevent the plate from cracking whilst drying and during firing.

If you are throwing a plate with a rim then the clay should be pushed out as far as the inside edge of the rim. At this point there should be enough clay around the edge of the disc to pull up vertically into a wide, shallow cylinder.

Continue to throw the plate by pulling the walls to the throwing gauge, continuing the cylindrical form. The throwing gauge should be set to this point rather than the point where the rim of the plate will eventually be.

With a pointed trimming tool, create an undercut that will eventually be used for guiding the wire underneath the plate. This is done at this point before the rim of the plate is created

With the wheel spinning at a steady speed, use a firm rib to fold the cylinder wall down to form the rim. It is important to maintain a continuous and even hand and wheel speed for this step. The wider the rim the more difficult this is.

Finish the surface and rim of the plate using a rib, sponge and chamois leather.

Finally, wire off the plate. Make sure that the wire is held taut whilst being dragged beneath the plate, as wide forms can drag the wire up into the clay, resulting in an over-thin base.

TROUBLESHOOTING COMMON FAULTS

S-Cracks: An S-crack could occur if the clay hasn't been compressed firmly enough on the wheel. If the plate has a flat base that is in full contact with the kiln shelf, then the movement caused by the shrinkage of the clay in the firing meeting the resistance of the kiln shelf, which doesn't shrink, can cause a stress crack. A good tip is to fire a plate like this on top of a fine layer of potter's sand.

Slumping: Depending on the clay used and whether or not there is adequate support, for example if you have only one foot-ring, the plate may slump in the firing. Ensure you consider this aspect in the design stages.

Warpage: If the plate wasn't removed from the wheel well, there could be warpage. Also make sure the kiln shelf is completely flat and not warped. Wide forms such as plates are particularly prone to warping when fired on kiln shelves that are not completely flat.

clay, where you are naturally controlling the consistency of the clay in the process of reclaiming it, is a useful option. Testing different clay consistencies to find your preference for a particular design is advisable. It is much easier to work with clay that has been thoroughly wedged and kneaded.

If you are working on a batch of plates, it can be useful to sacrifice your first plate of the session and wire it in half to examine the cross-section. If throwing a batch of plates that need to be regular in size and shape then using a throwing gauge with two arms is useful – one arm for the cylinder stage and a second arm set to the final position of the rim.

Whether you are trimming a foot-ring later or having a flat-bottomed plate, it is important to make sure the clay is the correct thickness across the base when still on the wheel. Using a set weight of clay and measurements to throw to will help with this. You can also use the needle tool, by pushing it vertically down to the throwing bat and using your finger to mark the depth, to see the thickness of your base.

BOWLS

There is so much to play with in the bowl form, with so many shapes and functionalities to consider. It can actually be tricky to know where to begin.

One of the challenges when throwing bowls compared to a simple cylinder is that the curved wall of a bowl will overhang the base, increasing the risk of the clay slumping under its own weight. To counter this there are a couple of steps the potter can take.

First, the less time with your hands on the clay the better. Try to make each movement count, as the more you touch the clay, the more water you add and therefore the clay will become more saturated, heavy and weak.

Second, think about the structure of the pot as you make it. If you make an initial curved bowl shape in the early stages of pulling the clay, and then continue to pull the clay in this shape to make it reach higher and wider, then it is more likely to slump and collapse. Instead, after making the curved base of the pot, move the clay in an S-shape so that it goes up and then out. Use this technique to extend the clay to your intended finished dimensions, then invert the curve into the final shape. This will mean that you are moving the clay into the correct shape rather than still trying to pull it in these final stages of throwing – this is the inversion technique. Alternatively, pull the walls of the bowl straight; the rim should have a narrower diameter and taller height than the final dimensions. Then start to make the curve of the bowl; as you do so, the diameter will naturally widen and the height will drop.

If you are planning to throw a small bowl with a narrow base then you can work directly on the wheel head and lift your pot off immediately when finished. However, if the bowl is going to be large or have a wide base, and be likely to distort if lifted by hand from the wheel, attach a bat to the wheel head.

As a bowl opens out on the wheel and is pulled wider, the speed the clay passes through your hands increases; therefore it is important to keep the wheel speed under control. As the bowl becomes wider, the wheel speed should become slower. Change the wheel speed between pulls, when you are not touching the clay; this helps prevent uneven wall thickness. As with all forms, maintain a consistent wheel speed and hand speed throughout each pull.

Once you have centred your clay, make a disc that is slightly wider than the intended base of the finished bowl.

Press down into the centre of the clay to create the base of the pot. Be conscious of the thickness of the base at this point – is the pot going to have a foot-ring or a flat base? Is there enough or too much clay?

Set the base of the bowl by opening up the clay in a curve. This will be the beginning of the bowl form so it is important to consider the shape of the curve you are making at this point. The opened-up clay should overhang the base of the pot to allow the outside hand underneath.

Position the outside hand at the base of the pot and the inside hand in the middle of the pot. Start moving the inside hand first and, when it's parallel to the outside hand, move them in tandem. The inside hand should be above, pushing the clay out slightly, and the outside hand should be below, pushing the clay back in slightly. Pull the clay upwards and out.

Through the next series of pulls, bring the walls of the bowl up in an S-shape until the required diameter and height have been reached. It's important to pull the clay efficiently with bowls. With the next pull, try to reach the required height, leaving enough clay in the walls for the following pull to make the width.

Now that the clay has been pulled to the right dimensions, correct the curve of the pot so that the S-shape is inverted to create the final bowl shape. You may wish to use a kidney-shaped rib on the inside of the pot instead of your fingers to do this. When judging the curve/shape of a bowl, attention should be paid mainly to the inside surface, as the outside will be trimmed later.

Using a metal or rubber rib, finish the inside and outside surfaces of your bowl, paying extra attention to the interior surface and shape. Use a chamois leather to finish the lip.

Trim away excess clay from the base using the square metal trimming tool; then, with the pointed trimming tool, cut a groove and lift the pot from the wheel either by hand or on a bat.

PULLING HANDLES

This demonstration is of a handle-attaching process on a mug. If following along, make sure that your mug bodies are evenly dried to leather hard and ready to trim. The first stage is to make handle blanks; these are pieces of clay that have been part-formed into straight lengths that will be later attached to a pot, and then continued to be pulled and shaped to form handles. Here we will be describing making a batch of handle blanks as we would when making a batch of mugs. However, you could equally use this method to make a single handle, or handles of varying scale.

There are also many other techniques for making handles, including slab rolling, extruding and casting, but the technique we will focus on is the traditional pulling method.

Pulling the Blanks

Prepare a piece of clay that can be gripped in one hand and, if making a batch, is large enough to create multiple handles from. Form the clay into a cylinder by patting between your hands or rolling on a work surface. Be careful not to work any folds or grooves into the clay; it should be as smooth and consistent as possible.

In one hand, hold one end of the clay, allowing the rest of the clay to hang vertically down. Then, using plenty of water on both the clay and your free hand, grip the clay at the top (just underneath the hand holding it) by creating an O-shape around the clay with your thumb and index finger.

Slide your hand down the length of the wet clay, and continue the motion past the end of the clay. It is important to maintain the shape of the 'O' created by your hand during each pull, otherwise the handle blanks will become uneven in thickness. Only apply pressure when you initially grasp hold of the clay. Each pulling motion extends the length of the clay further.

The shape of the 'O' is specific to each potter's hands, and will create a specific profile to the handle; however, through practice, this can also be controlled by the potter. I find that the shape of my hands creates a teardrop profile in the clay. To counteract this, I alternate the position of my hand on the clay, moving it around 360 degrees to create a round profile, or switching my position between 0 and 180 degrees to create an oval profile. Then, if you choose, the profile of the handle can be further defined by running your thumb or fingers down the length to create an indent or groove.

The aim is to stretch the piece of clay to create a length that is long enough to separate into multiple handles, all of the same consistent profile. Cut the pulled clay into individual handle blanks by laying a length of the clay perpendicular to a table edge, and cutting it off between the edge of the table and the side of your thumb that is holding the clay. Repeat this until you have the required number of handles (we generally pull a few spare blanks just in case any go wrong further down the line). If you wish to save the handles for later, whilst pots are being trimmed for example, place the handle blanks on a ware board and cover up with plastic whilst you trim the mug bodies.

Attaching the Handle

6 Mark on the mug the point you want the handle to be attached using a needle tool and score.

7 Gently hold a handle blank, with the surface that is going to be attached to the mug slightly protruding from the top of your hand. With the index finger of your other hand, press the clay so that the top of the handle opens out, creating a slightly larger surface area that will be in contact with the pot wall.

8 Score and slip this surface of the handle, and slip the pot that you have just scored, making sure that all the score grooves are completely filled with slip. Doing this causes both the handle and wall to bond securely, aiding a secure attachment.

9 With one hand supporting the inside wall of the pot, press the handle into place and carefully move it very slightly from side to side to make sure the slip grabs the handle onto the pot securely. You should see some slip appearing around the handle join – clean this away with a sponge.

10 Keep the handle straight at 90 degrees to the pot and, with a finger or modelling tool, smooth the join. The handle should now be firmly attached to the pot and ready to be pulled into its final shape.

11 Hold the pot with your fingers evenly spread around its base (this helps to avoid distorting the shape). Hold it over a pot of water with the handle left to dangle vertically down. With your free hand, using plenty of water on both the handle and your hand, continue to pull the handle until you are happy with its weight, consistency and profile.

Once the handle is pulled to the desired length, you may define its profile further by applying pressure through the pull with your thumb or fingers (or even your fingernails). A handle can also be tapered at this point by carefully increasing hand pressure through the pull. If at any point when pulling a handle you feel a lump at the end of the clay, just pinch it off and discard.

Change your grip on the pot so that you are now holding the mug with your thumb underneath the handle join and your fingers around the pot on the opposite wall. With the other hand (that has been pulling the handle), hold the end of the handle between your fingers and thumb.

Look down the length of the handle towards the mug body, then pivot the mug to begin the curve of the handle. Place the base of the handle in position and apply slight pressure so that it holds in place but would still be able to be moved if you need to change its placement.

The mug can now be moved freely to check the positioning and curvature of the handle.

When you are happy with the handle, pinch off the excess handle clay and press the clay securely at the base of the handle; smooth and clean up the joint if you wish. Any final adjustments can also be made to the handle's curve if required.

Place the finished mug on a clean ware board, and keep covered with plastic or in a damp cupboard for two days to even out the moisture within the entire pot and begin a slow drying process. This will reduce the chance of cracks appearing in the handle joint.

TIPS AND TROUBLESHOOTING

With practice and experimentation you will be able to manipulate the handle in a controlled and predetermined way. As with pulling the handle blanks, it is important to maintain a controlled grip on the clay throughout each pull, apply the pressure initially close to the join and maintain your hand shape without increasing or releasing pressure through the pull.

Throughout this whole process it is vital to keep the handle straight and at 90 degrees to the pot. If you don't support the handle at this angle then it will bend close to the joint and create a weak point, which will be exacerbated with each pull and could result in the handle appearing misshapen; the handle may even break apart when you are pulling it.

SPOUTS

Spouts can be technically difficult for a potter because sometimes they just don't pour well. Often we can master the perfect pour with our design, but the fact that each piece is made by hand also means there can be subtle variations and not all pieces pour equally. However, there are some general tips to help us along. It is important that the spout funnels the liquid effectively. The shape of the spout and body combined must create a cut-off point for the liquid. Too fast and the liquid will overflow; too slow and the liquid will dribble. Having a sharp edge at the mouth of the spout also helps aid the liquid in cutting off efficiently, and helps prevent liquid from running back down or dripping off the outside face of the spout while pouring. A sharp edge can be created in a few different ways, depending on the type of spout.

For a teapot, the drainage holes in the body, at the base of the spout, should help control the flow of liquid. Too few holes may stifle the flowing. Also with a teapot, the throwing rings inside the spout can cause the flowing liquid to swirl and bobble. The height of the tip of a teapot spout should be level with or slightly higher than the lid opening. If it isn't high enough then tea will spill from the spout before the teapot is full.

Throwing a Half-Cylinder Spout off the Hump

Create a groove for the wire to sit, just beneath the base of the cylinder, using a pointed metal trimming tool.

Roughly centre a piece of clay large enough to make your required number of spouts and re-centre the top point of the clay.

Begin to throw a small cylinder, being careful to create a base at your required depth. If you wish, callipers and a ruler can be used to check that you are throwing the cylinder to the correct measurements.

Stop the wheel spinning and wrap the wire into the groove; then slowly start the wheel and pull the wire through. The thinner and more flexible the wire the better – even a strong thread can be used for wiring off in this way.

Chapter 4 – Step-by-Step Making Processes 61

Attaching a Thrown Spout to a Jug Body

Have a leather-hard jug body trimmed and ready for a spout to be attached. Allow the spout cylinder to dry until it is leather hard. It should reach a point where the clay can hold its form yet still be manipulated slightly without cracking.

With a knife, cut the cylinder in half vertically.

Place each half on the newly cut edge and cut down to remove the unwanted clay from what was the base of the cylinder. This cut is creating the edge of the spout that will be attached to the body of the pot. You may wish to cut at an angle or curve so that the spout will fit the body of the pot and allow for liquid to flow.

Carefully hold the spout in one hand and, with the other, rub the clay so that the surface that is to be joined to the pot is made wider with a slightly rounded underside.

Mark on the jug body where the spout is to be attached, then score and slip both the face of the spout and the jug where they are to be joined.

Press the two components together and, with a sponge, remove excess slip. With your finger or a modelling tool, smooth the joint.

Using a sharp, fine knife, cut away the clay from the jug body creating the opening for liquid to flow out from; follow the shape and angle of the spout as you do so.

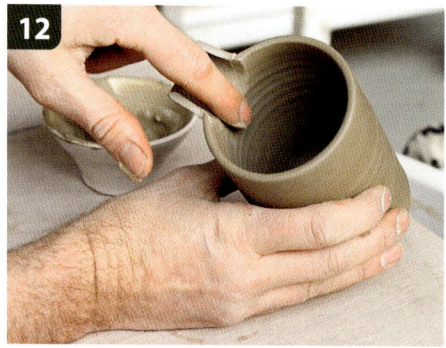

With a wet finger or sponge, clean up the inside joint and make it as smooth as possible to enable a clean flow of liquid.

To finish the jug, clean up and fettle the spout, and leave under plastic sheeting or in a damp cupboard to slowly dry.

Throwing a Jug Form and Pulling a Spout

A traditional jug form has a chamber for holding liquid, often a rounded shape, which is collared to create a neck that opens slightly to the lip of the pot where there is a spout. A handle is often joined from the lip of the pot to the widest part of the belly.

Start the process of throwing a cylinder. Allow for a little extra clay to be left in the walls to create the rounded belly with. The cylinder should be made to a little above the final height of the pot, as when the belly is created the height will reduce.

Focus next on shaping the belly by pulling the clay up and out to the height and diameter of its widest point; then as you move upwards to the neck, push the clay back in to create a round shape. All the clay doesn't need to be moved in a single pull, but try to be as efficient with your movements as possible.

To create the neck of the pot, the clay needs to be collared. At the point you want the neck to be, apply even pressure all around the pot and squeeze in. This can be done with evenly spaced fingers applying even pressure or by 'strangling' the pot with your fingers and thumbs wrapped around the pot.

Finish the shaping of the belly up to the neck of the pot. Continue to pull the pot from the neck to the lip. Using a sponge on a stick takes any excess water from inside the pot.

A rib tool can be used to finish the outside surface, defining the shape and removing excess water and slip.

Once the throwing is complete, move on to creating a spout in the lip. Use the index finger and thumb of one hand to support the outside face of the lip – the gap between the two fingers will become the spout.

Wet the index finger of your free hand and rub side to side along the inside face of the lip, gradually stretching out the clay. You may wish to stretch only the top of the lip, the entire wall of clay from the neck to the lip, or anything in between. The different variations that can be made will affect how liquid flows and pours from the jug as well the aesthetic design.

If you wish to control the flow further, there are a couple more ways you can do so. 1. The shape of the lip can be manipulated by placing the index finger of one hand in the spout and the other hand pinching in the walls of the lip around your finger to emphasise the spout shape.

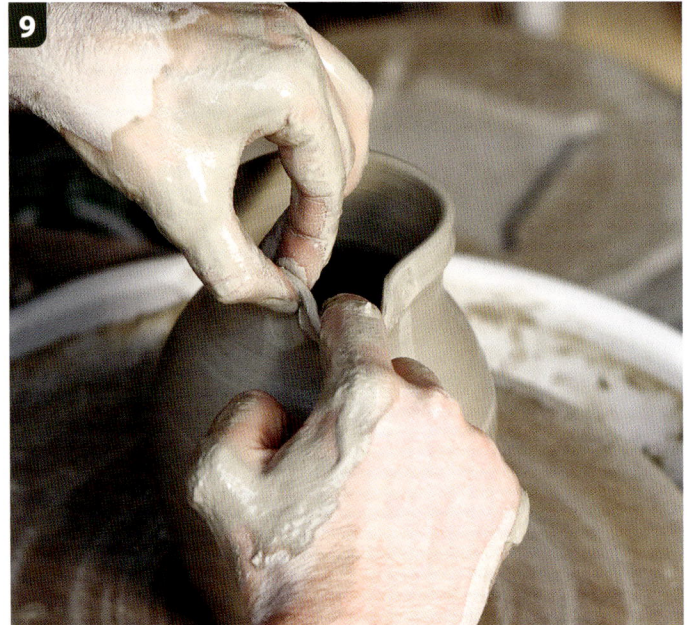

2. The clay either side of the spout can be stretched upwards by repeatedly pinching the clay slightly with wet fingers and pulling upwards.

The jug is now ready to be removed from the wheel and dried to a leather-hard consistency before having its handle attached.

Throwing a Teapot Spout

Before you start to throw the spout, consider the intended final shape and take into account the clay you will be discarding at a later point when the spout is cut at an angle. The thrown spout will be made with much more clay than in its final state.

Start by centring the clay and opening it out wide. The first couple of pulls should create a heavily tapered form.

With each pull, collar in the spout to keep the opening small. As the spout is going to end up being very narrow, the bottom half of the form must be worked on and finished before the cylinder of the spout is extended.

Move on to pulling the clay into thin walls to create a very narrow cylinder. You may need to use a modelling tool inside this cylinder instead of your finger. The inside surface of the spout should be as smooth and as free from throwing rings as possible to help with the smooth pouring of liquid.

If you are planning to cut the tip of the spout later then you can throw the spout longer, and don't need to worry about an uneven rim. With a kidney-shaped rib, finish the outside surface of the spout.

In this example, the spout has been thrown on a small bat that is now removed from the wheel to allow the spout to dry before being cut. However, if you are cutting and removing the spout at this point, hold a fine cutting wire (or a harp) taut between your hands and make a cut through the spout at an angle following the shape of the teapot body that it will be later attached to. Carefully wrap your hand around the spout so that the spout is protruding through the gap between your thumb and the base of your index finger. Then lift the spout and place on a ware board to dry to leather hard before attaching.

If, as in this example, you have thrown the spout on a bat that has been left to part-dry then the spout can be cut (as described in the previous step), and placed on a ware board until ready to attach. As the clay is thrown thinly, spouts can dry quickly so be sure to monitor and control their drying closely.

Attaching a Thrown Spout

Take a spout that has been partially dried to a soft leather-hard consistency. For the design in this example, the spout will be smoothed into the teapot body to give a fluid join, therefore the clay has to be malleable enough to work with whilst still being firm enough to hold its form.

Mark on the teapot the placement of the spout. To do this, wet the edge of the spout that will be soon attached to the teapot and lightly press it in place on the body of the teapot. Then remove the spout; left behind will be an oval-shaped trail of slip marking the place that the spout and body will be joined.

Within the marked-out area on the teapot body, use a hole-cutter tool to create a series of holes. The size, number and placement of the holes will have an impact on the flow of liquid from the teapot body through the spout; they will also act as a rudimentary strainer for loose tea leaves. Once cut, fettle the holes.

Take the cut spout and, with a lightly wetted finger, rub away any prominent throwing rings on the inside surface. This will help create a smooth flow of liquid as the undulation of the throwing rings can make the liquid bobble out of the spout.

Score and apply slip to both the edge of the spout and the area of the teapot body where they will be connected together. In order to create a strong bond between the two parts, make sure that the slip is well applied and all grooves are completely filled.

Firmly press the spout into place on the teapot body, being careful not to distort it. It is common for spouts to 'unwind' slightly during firing. As each potter throws slightly differently, the amount of movement is particular to each individual. To compensate for this, I position the spout with a slight rotation – if you imagine the tip of the spout as the hour hand on a clockface, I position it halfway between 11 o'clock and 12 o'clock. If you are making a cut into the tip of the spout then this should also be done at the same angle.

Remove any excess slip from around the spout join, and if as in this example you would like a seamless join, blend the clay of the spout and body together. You can use a sponge, modelling tools, your fingers or a combination of all these.

Once you are happy with the join, use a sponge to fettle the joint.

Now the spout is attached, the handle can be added to the pot. Be careful to monitor the drying closely – covering with plastic/placing in a damp cupboard or spraying with water as necessary – as the teapot and all its additions must dry slowly and consistently to avoid cracks appearing at joins.

LIDS

A well-fitting lid is a pleasing thing indeed. Lids can be tricky due to the precise nature in which they need to be measured and made; plus, the tendencies that some clays may have to warp and shrink can cause problems. That said, it is well worth the perseverance to create a pleasing lid.

Throwing a Body and a Lid

Throw the body of the jar. This example describes a simple cylinder form with the lip of the vessel acting as a gallery inside which the flange of the lid will sit, holding the lid in place. Measure the internal diameter of the jar using callipers. This measurement will be used when throwing the flange of the lid. For this design, a measurement of the external diameter of the lip also needs to be made as the lid will overhang the jar slightly.

Centre a piece of clay for the lid on a throwing bat and form into a disc, making sure it measures slightly more than the exterior diameter of the jar; it will be trimmed more accurately at a later stage. If this lid was going to sit inside a gallery on the jar then this measurement should fit the gallery dimensions instead.

The lid is being thrown upside down. In this step, the beginning of the flange is being created. Open out the clay to the inside measurement of the jar's lip, making sure that there is enough clay left in the base as the lid will be turned over when leather hard and trimmed. Take care to compress the clay thoroughly to avoid s-cracks appearing during firing. Then compress the outer surface of the clay to further define a ridge of clay that will become the flange.

Chapter 4 – Step-by-Step Making Processes

Pull up the ridge of clay to form the flange. As this will be trimmed when leather hard to create an accurate fit, the flange is being thrown slightly oversized. Depending on your design, you may choose to throw the flange as accurately as possible at this stage so that little or no trimming is required later.

Using the callipers set to the inside measurement of the jar's lip, check the measurement of the flange and adjust as necessary.

Compress the flange using a chamois leather and your fingers, and finish the surface of the pot.

Re-check the dimensions of your thrown lid and, if necessary, make any final adjustments. It is safer to have too much clay both for the total diameter of the lid and for the flange, as it can be trimmed to fit later.

Wire off the lid and set aside to dry. The lid is thrown much thicker than the body of the jar, therefore attention must be paid to the drying process so that when they are trimmed they are at the same consistency. When the lid is dry enough to not distort, remove from the bat and dry on a ware board. Cover with plastic if necessary.

Trimming a Lid

Centre the lid on the wheel with the flange facing upwards. For this example, I am using a chuck as it will protect the flange when the lid is turned the correct way round and the top face is trimmed. Alternatively, you can secure the lid directly to the wheel head to be trimmed and then, when turned the other way round, the top face can be trimmed whilst in place on the jar.

Place the finished body of the jar onto the lid to determine the amount of trimming required. You can also use callipers to take a measurement from the inside diameter of the jar's lip – this will be different from the measurement taken when throwing as the clay will have shrunk as it has dried.

As you trim away clay from the flange, keep placing the jar body onto the lid to check the fit – it is very easy to trim too much clay, resulting in a loose fit. The height and profile of the flange may vary depending on the function of the lid. For this example, the flange is relatively low, as its function is to keep the lid positioned in place, and has a slight taper. A lid for a teapot, for example, might need a much taller flange in order to catch the lid in the opening of the body, preventing it from falling out when the teapot is being poured from.

Once the flange of the lid has been trimmed to fit the body, spend some time finishing this face of the lid. Even though it will be (mostly) unseen, it is worth thinking about the finishing and how it impacts the aesthetic of the jar. For example, thought must be given as to how the lid and body will be glazed; will the lid be fired on the body? Will the inside surface of the lid be glazed? If so, edges, grooves and angles may need to be trimmed into the lid to aid the glazing process.

Place the body of the jar in position on the upturned lid. To hold the trimmed body of the jar in place without damaging the foot, place an upturned jam jar lid (or a trimming spinner) between the pot and your fingers. Turn away excess clay from the lid so that it just overhangs the lip of the jar.

Carefully remove the jar from the lid. This face of the lid is now complete.

Flip the lid over and re-centre on the chuck, so that the top face of the lid can be trimmed. Turn away the clay to your required design.

Finish the surface of the lid, removing any burrs from the edges.

Once the lid is finished, it should be placed on the body of the jar and they should be stored together as they dry. There is an overhang of the lid over the body, so the lid can be lifted off by gripping the edges. If your lid requires a knob, it can be added at this point – lids that sit inside a gallery or have no place to grip would need a knob adding.

Throwing a Knob on a Lid

Centre the trimmed lid on the wheel. In this example, I am using a chuck as it will protect the flange from being distorted. The lid may also be placed on the body of the jar, which in turn would be centred and secured to the wheel head. Score and apply slip to the centred point of the lid.

Take a small piece of prepared clay and carefully press the clay into the lid. The knob should be joined firmly to the lid, though care must be taken not to distort the lid at this point.

The knob can now be centred, just as a piece of clay that is to be thrown is centred, although a more delicate touch is needed. Try to avoid using too much water as this can saturate the leather-hard lid and cause it to slump or become misshapen.

Once the knob is centred, it can now be formed into the desired shape. In this example, I am making a small, solid knob, but there are many variations of size and design.

With the knob thrown, excess water and slip should now be removed from the lid and the surface re-finished.

Once finished, place the lid on the body of the jar and dry slowly in a damp cupboard or under plastic sheeting. With all components of the jar drying together at the same rate, distortion of the shape and cracks appearing in the join of the knob and lid should be prevented.

ASSEMBLING A TEAPOT – AN EXERCISE IN TIMING

We're using the teapot form here as an excellent example of one form that can encapsulate all the forms and techniques covered so far, and also to provide you with a timeline of actions that would typically happen in producing a complex form such as this.

The art of making a teapot is not only in the design and technique of the making but also in the timing and ability to control how quickly or slowly the clay dries. Teapots are usually made of four components: the body, handle, lid and spout. Each of these components needs to be made separately and constructed when the clay of each part is as similar in consistency to each other as possible. Problems start to occur when this is not the case; a lid that is at a different consistency to the body when trimmed and fitted together may fit perfectly at first, but as the clay continues to shrink throughout the drying (and then when in the kiln), the two pieces may end up not fitting together well at all.

Day One

Step 1: Throw the teapot bodies and lids. If the climate in your studio is cool and damp, also throw the spouts and cover well with plastic (these will dry out much quicker than the teapot bodies and lids), but if it is very warm, wait until the next day to throw your spouts.

Depending on your design, the lids may be thrown to fit each teapot specifically, that is, a lid with a flange that sits inside a gallery; or, if the lid and opening are to be trimmed to fit, then the lids can all be thrown to set measurements and fitted together when trimmed.

Step 2: Throw the chucks for the teapot bodies and lids to be trimmed on.

Step 3: Cover the pots as necessary for the next day. Sometimes we will create a damp cupboard out of plastic sheeting that allows the clay to dry very slowly, and leave it for the entire next day before continuing on day three.

Day Two

Step 4: Assess the firmness of the teapot bodies and spouts. They may need covering and/or spraying with water if they are drying quickly, or leaving out if still damp. Once the bodies have been dried enough to be handled without being distorted, turn the bodies and place them on their rims to dry the clay as evenly as possible.

Step 5: If the climate in the studio was too warm and dry on day one, throw the spouts now and leave them uncovered to dry.

Step 6: Pull the handles and lay them over a former, in this case a section of piping draped with a fine fabric, and monitor the drying.

Step 7: Trim the teapot bodies (preferably on a chuck).

Step 8: Trim the lids, either on a chuck or on each corresponding body as a chuck. If making in a batch, keep the lid in place on the body; this helps the two components dry at a similar rate and reduce the potential for distortion (when attaching the spout and handle, the lid will need to be temporarily removed).

Step 9: With a taut wire, or harp, cut the spouts at an angle at the point you would like them to be attached to the body.

Step 10: Mark on the body the placement of the spout. Then, using a hole-cutter tool, make holes in the wall of the teapot body within the marked ring where the spout is to be attached.

Step 11: Mark, slip and attach the spout (see the 'Attaching a Thrown Spout' step-by-step for further instruction).

Step 12: Once the handle has firmed up enough to hold its shape, but is still malleable, place on a template drawing, adjust the curve as required and cut the handle where the drawing dictates.

Step 13: Score and apply slip to both the teapot body and the handle, then attach the handle to the teapot body.

Step 14: Clean up with a sponge.

Days Three and Four

Step 15: Cover under plastic for at least two days to ensure that consistency of the clay evens out for the entire teapot and it begins to slowly dry. Continue to control the slow drying of the teapot to minimise the risk of cracks appearing at the joins.

Step 16: The teapots will be ready to biscuit fire when they are completely dry. After this point they will be ready to glaze and then fire again, processes covered in the upcoming chapters.

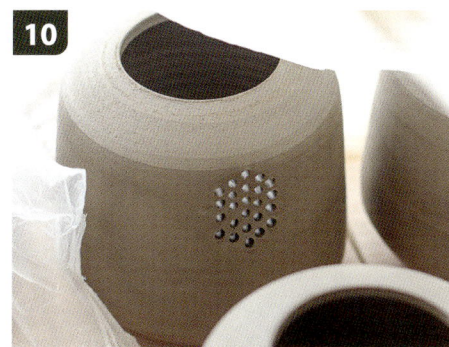

Chapter 4 – Step-by-Step Making Processes

CHAPTER 5

AN INTRODUCTION TO GLAZING

'As clothes are to the human body so are glazes to pots.'
                                                Bernard Leach

Creating your own glazes from raw materials is an extremely rewarding experience and also a great deal more cost efficient than buying pre-mixed glazes. It is personal preference whether or not you would like to mix your own glazes or use pre-made, but we would recommend getting to grips with at least the basics of glaze chemistry either way, as it will go a long way in understanding functional aspects of your tableware design.

In this chapter we are going to take a look at the more practical aspects of glazing; in the next chapter we will take a look at the chemistry behind ceramic glazes.

GLAZE PREPARATION

Here are our most commonly used items of equipment for glazing: a variety of sieves in different sizes and mesh sizes, glazing tongs, a mixer tool to add onto a drill, a fettling knife and needle tool, a variety of sponges and brushes, toilet brushes for mixing glaze, scales of different sensitivities, a hydrometer, a graduated cylinder and a syringe.

Glazing a ramen bowl.

USEFUL TOOLS

Sieves
It is useful to have a variety of sieves available in different sizes to suit different quantities of glaze being made. Also make sure you have different mesh sizes, commonly, 60, 80, 100 and 120. A narrow set of sieves is useful when producing small quantities of glaze tests.

Scales
Invest in a good set of scales that can measure to at least one decimal point. We would also recommend a smaller and more sensitive set of scales for when you are testing glazes in small quantities or weighing oxides, as the smaller the amounts you are measuring the greater the importance of utmost accuracy will be on your final result.

Sponges
When it comes to glazing, it feels like you can never have enough sponges lying around. A variety of shapes, sizes and materials is helpful.

Brushes
Similarly, it never hurts to have a plentiful supply of brushes for cleaning up glazed wares, applying glaze, applying surface decoration and so on. If you care for your brushes, they should last a great deal of time.

Tongs and Glazing Tools
Have on hand a few pairs and sizes of tongs. They can loosen and rust over time and need replacing. Other useful tools for glaze application are 'finger dips', a mechanic's car suction cup (for holding pots while dipping) and a plentiful supply of pouring vessels such as plastic jugs.

Plastic Buckets and Containers
You can never have too many plastic containers with lids. Purchase a set with securely fitting lids for big glaze batches and collect, gather and hoard as many containers as you can from elsewhere. Old ice cream tubs are often found in our studio, filled with glaze tests and slip experiments, plus raw materials that we consider to be safer to store in containers on a high up shelf.

HEALTH AND SAFETY

Many of the raw materials we use to prepare our glazes are hazardous to our health, either by causing airborne dust consisting of silica or being toxic and poisonous through inhalation, ingestion or, in a few cases, skin absorption. Always wear your respirator, making sure it fits properly with no gaps. It is important to clean up dust and spills with a damp cloth and never sweep. Dust extraction is a good idea if possible. Keep your raw materials in sealed boxes, clearly labelled and out of reach of children. Always add the raw material to water rather than the other way around, as this quells the dust. Wear gloves when glazing and have a set of clothes you wear just in the studio, changing out of them before going home, being sure to wash them regularly.

PRACTICAL APPLICATION

Some potters purchase pre-made glazes, which are usually sold in powder form and are added to water before the glaze is sieved and ready to use. In the next chapter, we will explore some basic glaze chemistry, but you can also start by going ahead and sourcing glaze recipes by other potters published in books or online.

If you are new to mixing your own glazes and are in the process of testing various recipes, it makes sense to keep the test sizes small, perhaps creating just enough in quantity to cover a few test tiles. Glaze recipes are usually listed with ingredients and a number that indicates the ratio needed. For example, 'potash feldspar, 40' would mean 40 parts out of 100 of potash feldspar. Occasionally, you may come across a recipe where the parts don't actually add up to 100 and you need to scale up the proportions so that they will add up to 100. To do this, multiply the amount of each ingredient, with the exception of the colourants (oxides, stains and so on), by 100 and then divide by the original sum of ingredients. After this point you can scale up the recipe to the required batch size.

Once you have your recipe in front of you with the desired batch size, you are ready to weigh out and prepare your glaze batch for either testing or production.

When it comes to applying glaze to a ware, there are many different methods. Which method you choose creates a different effect and attention should be paid to the water content of the glaze; for example, if brushing on a glaze it is likely to be a thinner application than dipping, and different forms require different lengths of time immersed in a glaze. It can be a hassle to have to alter the water content for a glaze for each different form. In our studio we work to an optimum specific gravity (which we will discuss in more detail in a moment) and if there is a form I know will

  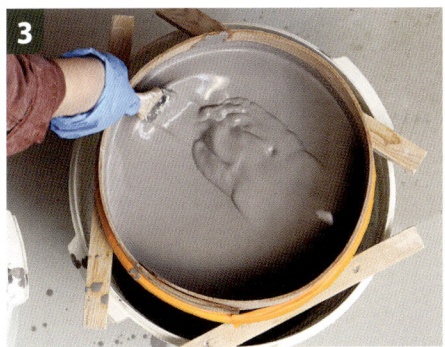

1. Fill your glaze bucket with water first, adding the raw materials into the water. This helps reduce the amount of fine airborne dust (always wear a mask). You can also place the lid over the bucket whilst you weigh out the next ingredient.

2. Once the recipe is weighed out, give it a mix and leave it to slake for a few hours, overnight if possible. Once you return to sieve it, use an electric drill with a mixer paddle to give it a really thorough mix. Failing that, a toilet brush is an excellent tool for mixing glaze.

3. The glaze now needs to be sieved. The mesh size you use depends on your preference but I normally sieve my glazes three times, first through a 60 mesh, then an 80 mesh and finally through a 100 mesh sieve. There are finer mesh sizes available, which would be used for any glazes that will be applied using a spray gun. You can use a brush or an old rubber rib tool to push the glaze through the sieve. You can also use old credit cards for this purpose. This is a very time-consuming task.

Adding red iron oxide wash over the top of a glaze. This will melt in the kiln and become much more fluid.

The result of the red iron oxide wash after it has been fired. This is a pale blue chun-type glaze, fired at cone 10 in reduction (*learn* more about reduction in Chapter 7).

need a thinner application – such as the holes on a teapot strainer (we don't want them to clog up with glaze), or the interior of a large bowl (which may have glaze sitting in it for a longer period while I glaze it) – I sponge lightly with water first so that the clay has absorbed more water and will therefore absorb less glaze. Hardly a scientific approach, but once you have experience it can work quite well. Some potters weigh their glazed wares and unglazed wares to determine the weight of glaze used. This data could be a useful tool for checking whether or not you are in the right ballpark if you are glazing something and it feels a little thicker or thinner than with previous batches.

1 Using tongs to hold a ware in place whilst dipping it in the glaze is probably the most common method of glazing in studio pottery. After glazing, it is a good idea to fettle away any marks left by the tongs.

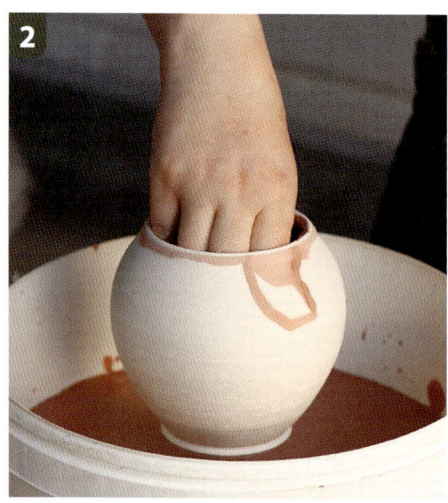

2 Often we dip pots into glaze. I have glazed the interior first, then used the outward pressure of my fingers to grip the pot whilst dipping it into the glaze to coat the exterior. If possible, glaze the outside of the pot quickly after doing the inside to prevent water saturation in the walls of the pot which will impact the thickness of the glaze applied to the exterior. Alternatively, you can wait until the following day to glaze the exterior, when the walls will be dry.

3 We often dip pots like this if they are for a test or if it is part of the design decision. It can be tricky to get a straight horizontal glaze lane when dipping pots like this but with practice it gets easier.

4 It is possible to brush glazes on too, though the application is often much thinner than when using tongs or dipping. Here a layer of glaze is being brushed over a different glaze.

5 Using a brush to add a textured layer of white clay slip onto the interior of a greenware pourer. Next this will be biscuit fired and then glazed in a celadon-type glaze, creating a brighter and more textured interior. Slip decoration can be used to a much greater degree to create pattern.

SPRAYING

Another technique for applying glaze is to use a spray gun and spray booth. The ware is placed in the booth and then a finely and evenly distributed layer of glaze is sprayed on. This technique often results in a much more perfect and uniform finish and is employed most commonly in industry. Glazes that are being sprayed need to be sieved through a mesh size of at least 120 so that the particles are fine enough.

RAW GLAZING

Interestingly, as energy prices fluctuate and such a lot of attention is on sustainability, some potters are returning to a traditional process of raw glazing, which means glazing directly onto greenware and skipping the biscuit firing stage. It is a skill to glaze a raw pot and it requires a high viscosity glaze, a careful hand and a much slower firing.

FETTLING

Once the wares are glazed, you will need to clean the bases, or the parts of the ware that will come into contact with the kiln shelf. Depending on how receptive your glaze is – some glazes just chip off at the slightest touch – you can use a small, sharp knife to fettle away any glaze drips.

Depending on the glaze, you may find some success at fettling away glaze drips before firing to achieve a more uniform surface. Sometimes it isn't possible – the glaze just chips off – and sometimes it isn't necessary, as the glaze has a good melt and the drip melts away. Perhaps you intentionally want to keep the glaze drips on the finished piece.

Potter Kim Lê explores the process of raw glazing and single firing in her project 'frugale', within which she is investigating more economically efficient modes of producing tableware. Single firing includes glazing greenware pots and skipping the biscuit firing entirely.

Chapter 5 – An Introduction to Glazing 79

DESIGN CONSIDERATIONS

While glazing is an overwhelmingly technical and scientific aspect of the overall production of wheel-thrown tableware, it is within the subtle and small design considerations that so much impact can be made and which in the end will inform a number of the technical decisions.

Colour, Texture, Function and Meaning

When working on a new design, often one of the first considerations to grapple with is colour. Unlike product design processes in other media, such as print, colour in ceramics is very much interlinked with other aspects of the glaze, for example texture and glossiness. A matt cobalt blue can be more vibrant than a glossy cobalt blue glaze, or a full gloss zirconium white is harsher than a matt tin white. A good way to achieve a pre-described colour is to use a mason stain with a chemically straightforward base glaze. Stains are fritted oxides and, when used with a simple glossy base glaze, are very reliable in creating the colour it describes on the tin. The drawback is that they are expensive and can lack a certain depth and character compared with using oxides.

Whether or not a glaze is glossy, matt, satin or something in between impacts the way the light absorbs or reflects on its surface, changing the way we perceive colour. It also affects our sense of touch. Many people distinctly dislike sipping out of a very dry matt-glazed mug, for example, while others do not mind. This is a functional consideration too. Glossy glazes tend to be chemically stronger and therefore more durable. A cup that is not fully glazed may suffer staining of the exposed clay, and similarly a very matt surface may discolour over time.

A great deal of meaning can be found in the way we choose to glaze our pots. Paying attention to create a harmonious nature between form and glaze, decisions about where to wax the foot to, applying surface decoration, and the thickness of the glaze are all things to consider. There are a great deal of decisions to be made and the tiniest detailed considerations often have an impact on the overall quality of the finished pot. It is also a process that can take many years of tweaking and trial and error in line with improvements in skill and knowledge.

Deciding on the Glaze Line

Where we decide to apply the glaze on the pot, whether right to the foot, at the very base, or to leave parts of the clay exposed, is part of both an aesthetic and functional consideration. Choosing to dip a mug, rather than wax the base and spend time wiping and cleaning it, can be a more straightforward process (although there is skill needed to dip well!). Arguably the mug has a more casual and homely feel to it. Whether or not you leave parts of the clay exposed can be considered too, depending on how your clay appears fully fired but unglazed. Unglazed clay may be difficult to keep clean from staining.

Applying wax resist to the foot of a pot, where the ware will typically meet the kiln shelf, is a very good idea. Not

The same form but one is glazed right to the base of the mug using tongs and the other is dipped. The dipped form has a slightly more informal appearance.

Applying wax resist to the base of a biscuit-fired mug to prevent glaze from adhering to the kiln shelf. Because we are using a pale stoneware, we have added some food colouring to the wax resist to help create a contrast between the clay and the wax.

only does it prevent glaze being absorbed by the ware and then wasted in the clean up, it speeds up the process and makes for a neater finish.

Playful Interventions

As part of the design process, it is good to try to understand the limitations or possibilities of a glaze. A good example to illustrate this is with a reduction glaze I use, which is incredibly runny if it reaches higher temperatures. I have worked to create a more stable version, but keep returning to the original formula for a couple of reasons, aside from the fact that it is beautiful.

First, from a practical viewpoint, it is a glaze that matures at cone 9 as opposed to cone 10 or 11, so I save pieces fired in this glaze for the cool spots of the kiln, such as the lower shelves, where cone 9 only just starts to bend. Second, I am able to achieve a certain aesthetic from the movement of the glaze by layering iron oxide brushwork over the glaze.

Similarly, I have developed a shino glaze that enjoys extremely hot temperatures, and so I save this for the pots that will go on the very top shelves of the gas kiln, where cone 11 bends.

Certain 'defects' can be subjective. Crazing (*see* 'Crazing' later in this chapter) and crackling glazes, for example, are exceptionally beautiful but strictly speaking not food safe because the structure of the glaze is weakened and over time will let moisture seep in and down through to the clay underneath. In actuality, this is rarely a hazard, especially when using non-toxic oxides and if the ware is fired and vitrified properly at cone 10. However, you may want to incorporate the beauty of a crazed glaze only on the exterior of a ware, using a liner glaze for the interior, which would hold food or drink.

Durability and Food Safety

Glazes have differing levels of durability and it isn't always easy to tell a durable glaze by appearance alone. When we talk about durability, we mean how strong and well-fitted the glaze is, as well as its capacity to endure the abrasive process of washing and being used over time. For tableware, durability is obviously important. When working with glazes and wanting to tweak existing formulas, it's important to stick to a few golden rules. One of the most important rules is to monitor the flux ratio, a topic we will cover in more detail in Chapter 6. This ratio is the relationship between the alkali metals and alkaline earth metals that make up the flux in the glaze. Research has demonstrated that the best ratio to use as a guide is 0.3 to 0.7. If you want to tweak elements of an existing glaze recipe, be sure that this flux ratio doesn't alter too much from the original recipe (if the original recipe has a strong flux ratio).

If your flux ratio is within this region and your glazes are properly matured (always use pyrometric cones in firings, even in an electric kiln), it is likely that your glaze will be safe and durable; however, it is a good idea to test it. There are some things you can do at home to test the durability of a glaze. Place a slice of lemon in the pot and leave it for a few days; if the glaze changes colour, fades, or discolours the lemon then your glaze is absolutely not durable and is actually leaching. This is hazardous because it means that the person using the pot is potentially ingesting the raw materials. Please note the lemon test only really works on extreme cases, and just because your ware appears to have passed this test, it doesn't necessarily mean it is food safe. Another good functionality test is to keep a piece in the dishwasher to see how it endures this incredibly abrasive environment.

You can also send off a sample to a lab and it is not too expensive. If you are selling work to the public, we would recommend you get your glazes professionally tested to this

A faceted beaker in a pale blue chun-type glaze. The glaze is intentionally quite runny so that the movement causes an interesting effect with the iron oxide brushwork over the top of the glaze.

British Standard. They will test for leaching. The British Standard only tests for lead and cadmium, but you can specify any toxins you would like to be tested.

If in doubt, use a reliable and safe glossy liner glaze on the interior of vessels and your other glazes on the exterior.

Specific Gravity and Viscosity

It is important to know how thick or thin to have your glaze and fortunately this is something we can easily control. This technical aspect is a design consideration and, whereas many potters approach the subject with a degree of nonchalance, for anyone hoping to create consistent, well-designed and well-made tableware, this is something to pay attention to. Over time, you'll come to learn the ideal consistency of your glaze and can be more exact at the weighing-out stage when you add the water. The more water added to the glaze, the thinner it will be. If a glaze is too thick, that is, it doesn't have enough water in it, it can cause defects, such as glaze pooling, crawling or cracking, because of the tension.

'Specific gravity' is a measurement of the density of a substance in comparison with the density of water, whereas 'viscosity' describes the interaction between the molecules in a fluid. For example, water has low viscosity and honey has high viscosity.

For potters, specific gravity can sometimes be a more useful tool of measurement for glaze consistency than viscosity due to the way in which raw materials can absorb water over time. To determine specific gravity, use a graduated cylinder to weigh the glaze, then divide the weight by the number of millilitres. You can use any vessel but a narrow cylinder or syringe is best for accuracy.

You can also use a hydrometer to measure viscosity, but, while being a useful tool to approximate the water content in a glaze, this doesn't tell us the density of a substance, only the thickness, and it can lead to inaccurate results. Over time, a glaze may gain a higher viscosity as a substance, for example clay absorbs water, but the specific gravity remains the same.

Glaze recipes don't usually dictate the specific gravity of a glaze, since it is often a matter of personal preference and circumstance. For instance, the temperature you biscuit fire to can impact the water content needed in a glaze, as can the glaze application method and also the desired aesthetic result. Therefore this is something that you yourself need to determine, usually through a process of trial and error. Although there are tools for determining accuracy with the consistency of the glaze, I always follow my instinct first, using the figures of specific gravity and hydrometer readings as a guide.

When a glaze is first mixed, it is a good idea to let it settle with the water for at least twenty-four hours before using it. This is so any soluble or absorbent ingredients can settle, as during the first few hours specific gravity and viscosity can change, albeit rather minimally.

It is preferable to start with your glaze being too thick as it is easier to add water to a glaze than it is to remove it (removing water from a glaze involves letting it settle for twenty-four hours and using a sponge or syringe to remove the water at the top). Many potters talk about a good consistency for a glaze as being like 'single cream' and this can be helpful in determining the first glaze consistency to test. In our experience, most glazes have a specific gravity of between 1.2 and 1.7.

Finding the Desired Specific Gravity

If you don't already know what your desired specific gravity is, then it is best to run a series of tests first with different quantities of water, each time calculating and recording the specific gravity. Once these are fired and you have analysed the results, you should be able to select the finish that works best for you and use that figure each time you make up a new batch of glaze. Sometimes this process can happen gradually, over many batches of making, tweaking ever so slightly each time. Taking time to establish the desired specific gravity is a valid step in the design process, even though it can feel time-consuming.

These three test tiles demonstrate the same glaze, but the glaze on the right-hand side has a higher specific gravity, meaning it contains less water and is therefore a thicker application, and the glaze on the left has a lower specific gravity. Whilst there is no golden rule and the choice is subjective, a glaze that is too thick or too thin can cause defects.

 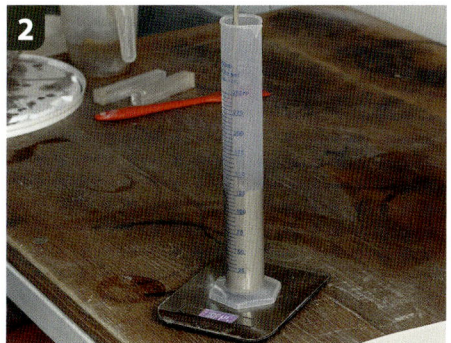 

Be sure to mix the glaze thoroughly using either a mixer paddle on an electric drill or a toilet brush – the latter is surprisingly effective. It is important to ensure all the water is equally distributed, and make sure you don't leave it even for a minute, as the raw materials can settle quickly.

Add the graduated cylinder and tare the scales, pouring in the well-mixed glaze to a level millilitre (it doesn't matter about reaching a specific quantity but in this instance I have measured out 250ml).

Divide the amount in grams by the amount in millilitres. The specific gravity for this glaze is 1.364 (339 divided by 250). The higher the number, the greater the density. If too thick, add a small amount of water and repeat all steps until the desired specific gravity is achieved. Once you are happy with the consistency, you can record this number and use it as a tool for measuring the consistency of the glaze at each use.

Flocculation and Deflocculation

A common and very frustrating problem with some glazes is that they have a tendency to settle into a solid mass at the bottom of the glaze bucket (this is known as 'hard panning' and means the glaze is deflocculated). Some glazes do this very quickly and some settle over time and can lead to time-consuming processes of mixing the glaze each time we want to use it. There are two reasons that this may occur. The first thing to check is whether or not you have enough clay in the formula to keep everything suspended. We would suggest that a good formula should contain at least 10 per cent clay, and if for whatever reason that isn't possible, adding 1–2 per cent bentonite is suggested. The process of flocculation and deflocculation concerns only the clay particles in your formula. The clay particles have a negative electrical charge, meaning that they repel one another as opposed to clumping together like the other raw materials. If there is no clay in your formula, this will be the problem and you should add 1–2 per cent of bentonite. This won't have much of an effect on the chemistry of the glaze but it will help to flocculate the mixture.

A word of warning though: if you simply add the bentonite to your wet glaze, it will have no effect unless re-sieved. A good way to incorporate bentonite is to sprinkle the desired amount over a small amount of water in a separate vessel and wait for it to slake down and become submerged. You'll notice how it becomes quite gelatinous. Then use a syringe or sponge to remove the surface water (discard the water) and then add the bentonite solution to your glaze. This ensures that the bentonite will become homogenised with the rest of the raw materials. Similarly, if you are weighing out your glaze formula (as opposed to fixing a hard-panning problem) and it contains bentonite, begin by adding this material to the water first, letting it slake down before adding the other raw materials.

However, if your glaze does contain clay – preferably in quantities of at least 10 per cent – and is still hard panning and causing problems, it is probably because it has become naturally deflocculated and adding more clay won't help. A great way to flocculate the glaze is to add saturated Epsom salts (magnesium sulphate) to the glaze. This will alter the viscosity of the glaze. Epsom salts are readily available in most supermarkets or online. By adding magnesium sulphate to the glaze, you are adding positive ions, which then attach to the edges of the clay particles. Now we have clay particles that have negatively charged faces, but positively charged edges, creating a lattice-like structure and thus suspending the glaze.

Before starting the process of adding Epsom salts to your glaze, make sure you have tested the glaze and recorded your desired specific gravity. Fill a container with warm water and start adding in the Epsom salts, stirring all the time so that they will dissolve. As soon as the salts stop dissolving, you'll know that the mixture is totally saturated.

Mix up your hard-panned glaze using a drill with a mixer paddle. If it is a really bad case of hard panning you may need to pour away the surface water into another container (to add it back in later), get your hands in there (wearing gloves) and break apart the clumped together particles. It may be a lengthy and frustrating process. While mixing the glaze, start adding a drop at a time of the saturated solution, stopping each time to see if the glaze has notably thickened. A glaze that is flocculated should coat your finger, feeling noticeably thicker.

As a general rule, try to establish the preferred specific gravity of your glaze before altering the flocculation of the glaze.

GLAZE TESTING

Achieving interesting, reliable glazes takes time and a lot of testing. A significant part of the testing process includes documenting your results. Make lots of test tiles so that it is quicker and easier for you to test glazes and record your findings, take photographs and keep notes.

Test Tiles and Plaster Moulds

In our studio we use different forms of test tiles to test different things. The easiest and most common way of producing test tiles is to throw a cylinder and then cut the tiles with a wire.

These standing tiles can be made quickly by throwing a baseless cylinder and cutting. As they are vertical, they are useful for demonstrating the flow of a glaze in a firing.

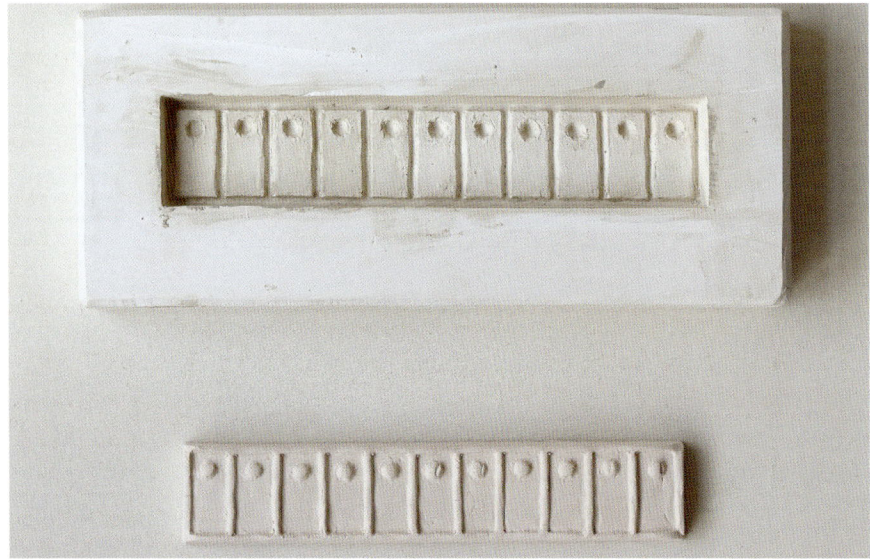

This is a really useful way of testing small amounts of glaze and running line blends to get initial results before testing further. We made a plaster press mould so we can easily make the test tile over and over again.

Small bowls or cylinders can be used to investigate a glaze further and see how it reacts on a three-dimensional form.

The cylinders each represent a different blend of two clays, but all with the same glaze applied. The left-hand cylinder is 100 per cent pale stoneware and the right-hand cylinder is 100 per cent grogged stoneware. The other cylinders are proportionate blends. It is a good idea to experiment with clay body as well as glaze.

We use a plaster press mould to create these flat test tiles. We use these less to test a glaze and more to send to clients and customers to describe an existing glaze to them.

Chapter 5 – An Introduction to Glazing

Line Blends

One of the quickest and most satisfying systems for unearthing a whole host of new results is to run a line blend of different glazes. The premise of this is simple:

These test tiles are the result of a line blend where I have investigated adding rutile to the formula in 2g increments. Rutile is the only ingredient being altered and it is interesting to notice how dramatic an effect this has upon the appearance of the glaze.

Test tiles resulting from a triaxial blend of the three glazes, all with the same base glaze but different colourant oxides. Notably tin oxide, manganese dioxide, cobalt oxide, red iron oxide and rutile. There are many browns but occasionally a very rich green or blue colour.

Working on a quadraxial blend, experimenting with three different mason stain colourants and rutile oxide but with the same base glaze.

I find it very useful to use reusable plastic cups and wooden lollipop sticks to weigh out my blends systematically and keep everything labelled.

to create a series of blends of a number of different glaze recipes. Line blends are often used to experiment with gradations of colourant oxide added, or to investigate the impact of one material in particular. Follow up all experiments by entering the quantities into your Unity Molecular Formula (UMF – this is covered extensively in Chapter 6) so that you can compare the surface appearance with the chemistry taking place. This is especially important if not just examining the work of colourant oxides or stains, but tweaking the quantity of flux, alumina or silica. Occasionally we can hit on a glaze effect we love by running a blend, but when we enter the figures into our UMF we learn it isn't very stable or durable. This is when the time-consuming work of tweaking and testing really kicks in. Some potters who devote a great deal of time to glaze development invest in a small test kiln so they don't need to wait for each time they do a glaze firing to test a glaze recipe. It's a great addition to your studio if you have the space and resource.

When running blends like this, a good tip is to use plastic cups to weigh out the glaze for each tile, create the allotted number of 'bases' and then use a syringe or measuring spoon to measure and sort the different variations. Sometimes the number of tests needed becomes huge – if running a triaxial or quadraxial blend, for example – so it can be prudent to run some of the figures through the UMF first, removing any configurations that just won't make the cut.

What to Do with Excess Waste Glaze

Our main gripe with glaze testing is the waste it can cause. We dislike throwing away precious raw materials and try to make use of our excess glaze tests where possible. If not possible to reuse, never tip them down the sink. Instead they must be dried out and disposed of responsibly.

Two good ideas for reuse are to simply add to one 'master' bucket to create a mystery glaze (if the tests contain enough red iron oxide this will likely turn out black or brown). Another thing is to dry out the tests, biscuit fire them, pass through a loose sieve and then add to an existing glaze in quantities of approximately 10 per cent. This will result in specks and flecks of colour within the glaze, which is incredibly fun!

TROUBLESHOOTING

Cutlery Marking

One of the most frustrating and common problems with glazes is cutlery marking, and this often occurs on industrially made ceramics too. In a chemically durable glaze, marks often happen when the surface is not smooth, for example with a matt glaze. The use of zircon to opacify a glaze, to make a white, for example, often causes marking. This is because the excessive zircon particles actually protrude (at a microscopic level) from the glaze. Another reason for marks is if a glaze is not fully matured. The answer to these problems would be to first of all find a compromise between aesthetic and function, if using a matt glaze for example. Second, ensure that you are firing your wares to the correct temperature. Third, if trying to opacify a glaze with zircon, run a line blend to see how little zircon you can get away with using to achieve a good opacity. I personally favour using tin oxide as an opacifier; however, it is incredibly costly in comparison. Also pay attention to ensure that there are adequate levels of alumina and silica in your glaze as this will help to increase strength.

Pinholes

Essentially, these are tiny holes that penetrate through the glaze and to the clay body. There is a great deal written about the causes of pinholing but much debate over its truth, so we will stick here to some practical methods we ourselves have found useful in thwarting this pesky problem. One thing we have noticed is that pinholes often occur on one clay body and not another with the very same glaze, so sometimes it is less a glaze problem but more a clay body/glaze relationship problem.

First, make sure all biscuit ware is clean from dust before glazing. Depending on your clay body, you may need to sand it (try to wet sand as it reduces harmful airborne silica). A very heavily grogged body does tend to do better with a pre-glaze sanding.

Another thing we have noticed is that pinholes often occur more on flatter surfaces such as plates and wide bowls. If this happens, it may be because the glaze is not fluid enough and you can try adding more flux to the formula.

Rutile can often cause pinholes so be cautious about the quantity you are using. Zinc can also contribute to this but calcining it first is said to help.

Soaking at top temperature in the glaze firing often helps too – for fifteen to thirty minutes. You can also experiment with increasing the temperature of your biscuit firing to make the biscuit ware a little less porous, but be aware that this may alter the required specific gravity for any glazes you use.

Crazing

Crazing is a glaze/clay body fit problem that occurs when the glaze comes under tension. This can happen immediately in and after the firing, or over the course of many years. A great many wares from very respected potters, particularly those who woodfire, are crazed and even more beautiful for it. However, crazing does mean structural weakness in the finished ware and that is a cause for concern – and what if our glaze does contain harmful materials, such as cobalt? When we design tableware, we want it to be durable and not prone to breakage and we certainly want it to be safe to use.

Crazing is relatively easy to remedy. First of all, we can plot our formula onto the Stull Chart (*see* Chapter 6) after we have established its UMF. This will give us an indication of whether or not it will fall in or near the crazed regions of the chart. If it does, try adding increments of silica and alumina in order to move the plot further away from the crazed region. Another thing to take note of is whether or not the formula contains too great a quantity of sodium and potassium, as these are high expansion and can cause crazing. Crazing can also occur if the glaze application is too thick, so take care with that. And be sure that the glaze is fully matured by always using pyrometric cones in the firing.

Shivering

Shivering is the opposite of crazing in that the problem is caused by compression as opposed to tension in the glaze. Similarly, it is a glaze fit error and can also be remedied.

Detail of a wood ash glaze with high amounts of feldspar. This piece has been wood fired and is exceptionally beautiful, though not very durable.

I have never had a case of shivering – it is relatively rare, as most glazes have a higher thermal expansion than glaze bodies. The remedy here is to increase the levels of potassium and sodium in the glaze, which both have a high expansion (and therefore are often prone to causing crazing).

Crawling

Crawling is an interesting defect; in fact many potters create intentionally crawled glazes that are just so beautiful. However, when it isn't intentional and when on a functional ware, it is just plain annoying. It is caused by surface tension in the melting glaze and can sometimes be caused by application errors or having too much clay in the glaze and not enough flux. Some fluxes such as zinc and magnesium contribute to crawling and so should not be used in excess.

Blistering

Blisters often are the result of a very thick glaze application or inadequate clay preparation but in our experience are also due to soluble ingredients in the glaze, such as soda ash. These soluble ingredients contribute much drama and beauty in a shino glaze, for example, but can also cause defects, so consider carefully whether or not to use this on a functional ware.

Detail of a shino-type glaze with crawling. In this instance, the crawling was a welcome defect, but often it is not. Many shino glazes are prone to this defect and are considered to be special effect glazes.

Row of espresso mugs thrown in a flecked stoneware and glazed in the same base glaze but with varying colourant oxides, developed over a series of years.

CHAPTER 6

UNDERSTANDING GLAZE CHEMISTRY AND RAW MATERIALS

As a student at school, chemistry was never the subject that caught my imagination. Since becoming ceramicists, however, we have learnt more about chemistry than in all the years at school, and overwhelmingly we now appreciate that chemistry is all around us and it is beautiful. The periodic table, devised by Russian chemist Dmitri Mendeleev in 1869, is a sophisticated, beautiful and functional system, and one of which we have only just come to appreciate. Some readers may already be well acquainted with chemistry and we hope that this chapter will still provide some useful information, but for readers who, like me, prefer to learn through practical application, this is for you and we hope you enjoy it.

We would like to state at the beginning that everything written in this chapter comes from our own experience but also many books and courses written by people extremely knowledgeable in the subject; we have provided reference to these in the Bibliography and Further Reading section at the end of this book.

WHAT IS A GLAZE?

A glaze can be likened to a glass skin covering the surface of the fired clay body. This surface provides protection and durability but also adds visual interest in the form of colour and surface texture. With functional ware it is the main point of contact between the food and the ware and so it is important that it is durable and food safe. It is possible to produce a pot without a glaze. One would simply fire the form unglazed and the form would be vitrified (if fired properly). However, the texture would be relatively rough, prone to staining and far less durable for food use.

Teapots glazed but not yet fired.

A clay blend series with a shino-type glaze.

Teapots after being glaze fired.

USEFUL DEFINITIONS

Element: A substance that cannot be broken down into other substances. Each chemical element is distinguished (as per the periodic table) by the number of protons in the nuclei of its atoms. This is known as the atomic number.
Atom: The smallest particle of an element that can exist.
Molecule: A group of atoms chemically bonded together.
Molecular weight: This is the weight of the atoms in the molecule.
Mole: This is the amount of substance, in grams, that is equal to its molecular weight.
Chemical reaction: When substances combine to make a new substance with different properties, weight and appearance.
Oxide: An element combined with oxygen. Many of our raw materials are oxides.
Stull Chart: This is a graph that was created by R.T. Stull in 1912. It plots the SiO_2 (silica) and Al_2O_3 (alumina) levels of a glaze recipe. It is useful to plot a recipe on the chart to predetermine whether or not a fired glaze will be glossy, matt, crazed or under-fired.
Unity Molecular Formula (UMF): Also known as the Seger Formula. The proportions of a glaze recipe in molecules rather than weights.
Primary flux: Also known as the alkali metals or R_2O, found in the first column of the periodic table. Lithium, sodium and potassium.
Secondary flux: Also known as alkaline earth metals or RO, they appear in the second column of the periodic table (with the exception of zinc). Magnesium, calcium, strontium, barium and zinc.
Flux ratio: The proportion of primary and secondary flux or $R_2O:RO$. Historically and generally (with the exception of some special effect glazes), the most reliable and durable ratio is 0.3:0.7.
Matt: A glaze finish that doesn't appear glossy.
Eutectic: The point at which a mixture of substances melts at a temperature that is lower than the melting points of the separate constituents.

Glazes are mixed from raw materials in powder form and added to water where the powder is suspended. Once the glaze interacts with the biscuit-fired or raw pot, which is usually dipped in or sprayed with the glaze, the water is absorbed like a sponge, leaving a powder coating of glaze on the surface. The glazed ware is then fired in the kiln and, with the application of heat and time, the glaze matures, melts and forms a durable surface.

It is incorrect to think of the body of the pot and the glaze as something materially different. In fact, the raw materials that are combined to make a glaze formula are also commonly found in the clay body. The two parts have a relationship and different glaze recipes fit differently to each clay body. I find it helpful to think of clay body and glaze as being two cogs in the same machine, working together to create one fluid piece.

But what actually is a glaze? A glaze formula can be made out of many ingredients but to be successful in its job these raw materials need to contain silica, alumina and a flux. Interestingly, many primitive glazes are made from raw clays and wood ash, since these humble, abundant materials contain everything we need to make a durable and successful glaze.

Silica, Alumina and Flux

Silica (silicon dioxide) is a substance found in most rocks. It is present in the clay we throw with and, in our glazes, it is known as the 'glass former'. Typically, the silica in our glazes is sourced in materials such as flint, but, being so abundant, is found within many, in fact nearly all, other raw materials we are using.

Alumina is found within all glaze formulas and is one of the major substances within the clay body too. We use alumina to give our glazes tensile strength and body. It also helps to keep the glaze particles suspended and prevent too much movement in the melt. By altering the ratio of silica and alumina in a glaze, you can control whether the glaze is glossy or matt. Alumina is typically found within the clays we add, such as ball clay and kaolin, but also in raw materials such as feldspar and nepheline syenite.

A key premise of glaze chemistry is the fact that the melting point of silica is 1710°C (3110°F) and the melting point of alumina is 2072°C (3761.6°F), which is notably hotter than our kilns are able to reach. Therefore in order for the glaze to transform from the powdery raw surface that we apply to the biscuit ware into a smooth, glassy, durable glaze, it needs to melt. A cone 10 firing temperature typically reaches 1260°C (2300°F). Here lies an essential building block of glaze composition – the fluxes.

The fluxes are oxides that work with the silica and alumina to lower the melting point of the glaze. Most fluxes, when fired individually, don't work this way and it is only when combined with substances such as alumina and silica that they interact with the molecular structure to lower the melting point. The process of combining materials to alter the melting point of a substance is called eutectics. The fluxes also impact the colour and texture of the glaze.

The fluxes can be categorised into two groups: alkali metals (R_2O) and alkaline earth metals (RO).

Alkali metals can typically be found in the first column of the periodic table, for example, sodium, lithium and potassium. These are very powerful fluxing agents and they also have impact over the colour of the glaze. These are often called primary fluxes.

Alkaline earth metals are often, but not always, found in the second column of the periodic table. These are often called secondary fluxes as they are less reactive than alkali metals (primary fluxes); however, they have a more instrumental role in contributing to the durability and hardness of the glaze.

A great deal of attention should be paid to the ratio of these two fluxes as this is where much of the ability to create a durable and food-safe glaze lies. Research shows that a flux ratio of 0.3 R_2O:0.7 RO is the ideal figure. We will explain this in more detail a little further on in the chapter. There is some wiggle room, but this is a good ratio to aim and plan for as a general rule. Some special effect glazes follow a different rule, but most functional glazes will have this ratio.

OVERVIEW OF COMMON RAW MATERIALS

Sourcing Materials

One of the biggest problems for small-scale potters is that many of our raw materials are not locally sourced. Indeed, many are by-products of larger-scale industrial mining. While being a small cog in the machine, it is still a good idea to consider the provenance of your materials. In the first instance, try to use raw materials that are local and question the necessity of using a raw material that comes with a lot of air miles. Sometimes it is difficult for us to establish the provenance of the material, but we recommend contacting your pottery supplier as they are very knowledgeable. Some materials have complicated contexts, such as cobalt, which is irreplaceable for creating those vivid blues but is often gathered using exploitative labour.

A useful activity to prepare yourself for working with glazes is to first of all familiarise yourself with common raw materials. One of the first experiments I did when exploring raw materials was to fire each raw material in the kiln and assess how they looked: did they melt? What was the colour, and so on? Raw materials are from the earth and they are finite, and because of this they change depending on where they are mined or collected. Ball clay from one supplier might not have exactly the same chemical composition as ball clay from another, although it might be similar. You should be able to obtain the exact chemical analysis from your supplier.

Alumina

Kaolin/china clay is a primary clay (meaning that it is a clay that has not travelled from the parent rock via erosion or water), and it has little plasticity. It is often used in the composition of prepared clay bodies. In a glaze, it is used to provide alumina and silica.

Ball clay is a source of alumina and silica. Ball clays are usually very flexible, plastic and high in silica. Unlike china clay, ball clay is a sedimentary, or secondary, clay, which is why it is so plastic.

Bentonite is a source of alumina and silica, often used to create durable surfaces and improve glaze suspension.

Silica

Silica is the main glass former in a glaze and can be sourced in materials such as flint and quartz. As silica is so abundant, it is often found in trace amounts or as secondary sources in materials such as feldspar, clay, talc, wood ash and various frits (frits are fluxes that have already been melted and ground to a powder).

Feldspars

Feldspars are very abundant minerals. Potters use feldspars containing sodium and potassium as fluxes in a glaze. Cornish stone, as the name suggests, is a crushed stone consisting of many different components and fluxes, including potassium and sodium. It is a low iron flux, historically mined in Cornwall but nowadays pottery suppliers make the same composition by combining other feldspars.

Potash feldspar is a source of potassium, sodium, alumina and silica. This is one of the most commonly used fluxes. If used in high quantities it can cause crazing.

Soda feldspar is a source of potassium, sodium, alumina and silica. Soda feldspar is found within a mineral called albite. White in appearance, it is used in a similar way to potash feldspar.

Nepheline syenite is a source of potassium, sodium, alumina and silica. It is lower in silica and higher in alumina than potash and soda feldspars. It is commonly mined in Canada and Norway.

Magnesium

Talc is a source of magnesium, silica, calcium and alumina that can be used as a secondary flux. Used in small amounts, talc can help to prevent crazing as it has a low thermal expansion. Dolomite is a source of magnesium and calcium, used as a secondary flux. Used in small amounts, dolomite can help to prevent crazing as it has a low thermal expansion.

Calcium

Whiting, otherwise known as limestone, is a source of calcium. It can be used as a strong flux in high temperatures. Wollastonite is another alternative calcium mineral that can be used in place of whiting. While being quite similar in chemical composition to whiting, it is sometimes favoured by potters as it emits no carbon dioxide bubbles (whiting emits carbon dioxide in the firing) and may therefore, arguably, lessen the number of pinholes in a finished glaze.

Boron

Boron is most commonly found in a material called colemanite and Gerstley/Gillespie Borate. Colemanite is an insoluble source of boron and is used as a powerful flux that can intensify colours. Frits containing boron tend to be less soluble and act as strong glass formers.

Zinc

Zinc oxide is often used as a flux in mid-temperature glazes.

Barium and Strontium

Barium carbonate is used in some high temperature glazes as a flux and is well known for enabling vivid turquoise colours when combined with copper. It is highly toxic. A non-toxic source flux with very similar properties is strontium carbonate.

Wood and Plant Ash

Ash from burning wood and plants is a very traditional glaze material. As the plant grows, it draws various minerals from the earth and these survive in the ash, enabling lots of interesting chemical opportunities in a glaze. Typically, wood and plant ash is a source of silica, alumina, calcium, potassium, phosphorous, magnesium and iron. Some woods are known for unique effects, such as apple, which can be a vivid green. Grasses and reeds tend to be high in silica.

A wood-fired bowl, glazed in a wood ash glaze, consisting of ashes from willow and ash trees, with iron oxide brushwork.

COLOUR

The colour of the glaze is defined by a few variables. The most straightforward way to add a predetermined colour is to use a stain. These can be added in various percentages, usually specified by the manufacturer. Stains are manufactured powders composed of oxides that help stabilise the colour.

Many potters use oxides to add colour. They are cheaper than purchasing stains and can enable greater creative control. One thing to bear in mind is that stain and oxide colour will appear quite differently depending on the other materials used in the glaze. Different fluxes, whether or not the glaze is glossy or matt, all have a part to play in the colour formation.

Common Colourant Oxides

Iron
Iron is such a fascinating and abundant oxide to use as a colourant in glazes. There is trace iron in so many of our raw materials and clay bodies; in fact, many materials go through processing in order to reduce amounts of iron present. In oxidation, it produces mainly browns and yellows, and in reduction is responsible for pale blues and greens. It can be added in the form of red iron oxide, black iron oxide and yellow ochre. These are similar substances but do in fact differ in terms of concentrations and mesh sizes. Red iron oxide is a refractory material and most commonly used in glazes. Black iron oxide actually performs more as a flux and is the strongest concentration of iron. Yellow ochre is the weakest concentrate of iron.

Cobalt
Cobalt is well known for creating intense blue colours, but in fact can contribute to many different colours. It is added to glazes as either cobalt oxide or cobalt carbonate (cobalt oxide is 1.4 times the strength of cobalt carbonate). Unlike iron, there is no impact on colour when firing in reduction or oxidation.

Nickel
Nickel is most often used in combination with other oxides and in small quantities. It is quite refractory and adding too large an amount can lead to glazes feeling dry. It is often used to create greens and greys.

Copper
One of the earliest raw materials sourced and used by humans, copper is a common colourant in glazes. It is very sensitive to oxidation and reduction atmospheres, and colours can range from green and turquoise to black and red – it really is quite versatile. It is often used in the form of copper carbonate, as this melts well in glazes. It is really important to ensure that glazes including copper are food safe and do not leach.

Manganese
Most often used in the form of manganese dioxide, manganese produces blacks, purples, pinks and browns. If used in high quantities, it produces metallic-appearing glazes. It is very toxic so must be handled with care.

Rutile
This is a source of titanium and often contains impurities, notably iron. Often there is a choice between light and dark rutile – dark simply contains more iron. Rutile is often used in glazes to help form crystals.

Tin
Tin is most often used as an opacifier and whitener, but also enhances colour in copper reds and chrome pinks.

Zircon
Zircon is also used as an opacifier in glazes and is commonly used in industry for creating ceramic tiles. It is cheaper than tin to use as an opacifier but can sometimes be prone to cutlery marking on its surface.

DETERMINING THE UNITY MOLECULAR FORMULA

When it comes to understanding glaze formulas, or if you would like to develop your own recipes, understanding how to read the UMF (also known as the Seger Formula) and the Stull Chart is of great use. The UMF is a method used to convert glaze components into the number of molecules and normalising the fluxes to a unity of 1.0. By unifying the fluxes, we can more easily compare the other parts of the glaze, such as the glass formers (silica) and stabilisers (alumina) as well as the other oxides added as colourants.

Recipes and formulas are often talked about in much the same way, but it is useful to differentiate the two meanings. A recipe includes a list of materials and percentage weights, but a formula is the chemical analysis of the recipe. This is important because with the chemical formula, substitutions for materials can be calculated. For example, a recipe may refer to a raw material that is no longer available to buy, or is hard to source in your country, or perhaps you just don't want to use it – in many cases a viable alternative can be found by using the chemical formula.

Case Study
One of the simplest glaze recipes you can make is the '4321' glaze which contains 40 parts feldspar, 30 parts flint, 20 parts whiting and 10 parts clay – this is a durable cone 10 glaze for stoneware. Let's take a look at this glaze recipe through a chemistry lens to see what is happening. Please also *refer* to the Bibliography and Further Reading section to find details of the Ceramic Materials Workshop courses, which provide lots of further information about the UMF and understanding glaze chemistry. You can use online calculators for this entire process and we would encourage you to do so (Glazy has a good one), but for the purpose of understanding the process, it is good to do it yourself a couple of times.

Recipe

Material	Amount
Potash Feldspar	40
Flint	30
Whiting	20
Kaolin	10

The '4321' recipe is a well-known simple and durable glaze recipe.

Step 1: Insert chemical composition

Material	Amount		Silicon dioxide	Aluminium oxide	Sodium oxide	Potassium oxide	Calcium oxide
			SiO_2	Al_2O_3	Na_2O	K_2O	CaO
Potash Feldspar	40	Chemical composition (%)	65.8	18.5	4	11.3	
Flint	30		98.54				
Whiting	20						56.03
Kaolin	10		50	35			

The first step in this process is to determine the chemical composition of the ingredients in the recipe. This information should be available via your pottery supplier, or if not there is a generic list on Glazy – it may not be the exact analysis of your material but it will be close enough. The easiest way to process this information is to create a table, either hand-drawn or on a computer, with the name of the raw materials on the left and the oxides at the top. For example, in potash feldspar, according to our supplier, we have 65.8 per cent silicon dioxide (SiO_2), so we have included this in the table. You will notice the percentages of the chemical composition of your materials don't always add up to 100 per cent and this is because the other parts will be released during the chemical reaction in the firing or are in such small quantities that they hardly impact the chemistry.

Step 2: Insert the molecular weight

Material	Amount		Silicon dioxide	Aluminium oxide	Sodium oxide	Potassium oxide	Calcium oxide
			SiO_2	Al_2O_3	Na_2O	K_2O	CaO
Potash Feldspar	40	Chemical composition (%)	65.8	18.5	4	11.3	
Flint	30		98.54				
Whiting	20						56.03
Kaolin	10		50	35			
Molecular Weight (g/mol)			60.08	101.96	61.98	94.2	56.08

Find out the molecular weight of each oxide and insert it into the bottom of the table. This is something that can be looked up online or in a book, as the molecular weight does not change.

Step 3: Work out the proportions

Material	Amount		Silicon dioxide	Aluminium oxide	Sodium oxide	Potassium oxide	Calcium oxide
			SiO_2	Al_2O_3	Na_2O	K_2O	CaO
Potash Feldspar	40	CC (%)	65.8	18.5	4	11.3	
		Proportion	26.32	7.4	1.6	4.52	
Flint	30	CC (%)	98.54				
		Proportion	29.562				
Whiting	20	CC (%)					56.03
		Proportion					11.206
Kaolin	10	CC (%)	50	35			
		Proportion	5	3.5			
Molecular Weight (g/mol)			60.08	101.96	61.98	94.2	56.08

The chemical information just inserted into the table does not take into account the proportions of your glaze recipe, which now needs to be worked out. Add a row underneath each material analysis and multiply the oxide percentage number by the raw material amount in the recipe. For example, in this recipe we have 40 parts potash feldspar, so we multiply the silicon oxide percentage for that material (65.8) by 0.4 (40 ÷ 100) to get 26.32. We would then do the same for each oxide (SiO_2, Al_2O_3, Na_2O, K_2O) on the potash feldspar row. For flint, we would multiply by 0.3 (30 ÷ 100), and so on.

Step 4: Total the oxides

Material	Amount		Silicon dioxide	Aluminium oxide	Sodium oxide	Potassium oxide	Calcium oxide
			SiO_2	Al_2O_3	Na_2O	K_2O	CaO
Potash Feldspar	40	CC (%)	65.8	18.5	4	11.3	
		Proportion	26.32	7.4	1.6	4.52	
Flint	30	CC (%)	98.54				
		Proportion	29.562				
Whiting	20	CC (%)					56.03
		Proportion					11.206
Kaolin	10	CC (%)	50	35			
		Proportion	5	3.5			
Molecular Weight (g/mol)			60.08	101.96	61.98	94.2	56.08
Total			60.882	10.9	1.6	4.52	11.206

The next task is to total each of the oxides. Create a new row in the table for this. To do this we need to total the numbers from the proportional row in each column.

Step 5: Convert into moles

Material	Amount		Silicon dioxide SiO₂	Aluminium oxide Al2O3	Sodium oxide Na₂0	Potassium oxide K₂0	Calcium oxide CaO
Potash Feldspar	40	CC (%)	65.8	18.5	4	11.3	
		Proportion	26.32	7.4	1.6	4.52	
Flint	30	CC (%)	98.54				
		Proportion	29.562				
Whiting	20	CC (%)					56.03
		Proportion					11.206
Kaolin	10	CC (%)	50	35			
		Proportion	5	3.5			
Molecular Weight (g/mol)			60.08	101.96	61.98	94.2	56.08
Total			60.882	10.9	1.6	4.52	11.206
Mole			1.01335	0.10690	0.02581	0.04798	0.19982

A mole is the term for the amount of a substance, in grams, that is equal to its molecular weight. In order to work this out, create another new row in the table, divide the sum of the oxides by the molecular weight per each material.

Step 6: Sum the fluxes

Material	Amount		Silicon dioxide SiO₂	Aluminium oxide Al2O3	Sodium oxide Na₂0	Potassium oxide K₂0	Calcium oxide CaO
Potash Feldspar	40	CC (%)	65.8	18.5	4	11.3	
		Proportion	26.32	7.4	1.6	4.52	
Flint	30	CC (%)	98.54				
		Proportion	29.562				
Whiting	20	CC (%)					56.03
		Proportion					11.206
Kaolin	10	CC (%)	50	35			
		Proportion	5	3.5			
Molecular Weight (g/mol)			60.08	101.96	61.98	94.2	56.08
Total			60.882	10.9	1.6	4.52	11.206
Mole			1.01335	0.10690	0.02581	0.04798	0.19982
Sum of the fluxes					0.27362		

Using the number from the mole calculation, add up all the fluxes. It may be useful to refer to the periodic table here. Remember that the fluxes include lithium (Li), sodium (Na) potassium (K), magnesium (Mg), calcium (Ca), strontium (Sr), barium (Ba) and zinc (Zn).

Step 7: Determine the UMF

Material	Parts		Silicon dioxide SiO$_2$	Aluminium oxide Al$_2$O$_3$	Sodium oxide Na$_2$O	Potassium oxide K$_2$O	Calcium oxide CaO
Potash Feldspar	40	CC (%)	65.8	18.5	4	11.3	
		Proportion	26.32	7.4	1.6	4.52	
Flint	30	CC (%)	98.54				
		Proportion	29.562				
Whiting	20	CC (%)					56.03
		Proportion					11.206
Kaolin	10	CC (%)	50	35			
		Proportion	5	3.5			
Molecular Weight (g/mol)			60.08	101.96	61.98	94.2	56.08
Total Proportion			60.882	10.9	1.6	4.52	11.206
Mole			1.01335	0.10690	0.02581	0.04798	0.19982
Sum of the fluxes					0.27362		
UMF			3.70350	0.39071	0.09435	0.17536	0.73029

To determine the UMF, divide the mole of each material by the sum of the fluxes.

	SILICA	ALUMINA	FLUXES		
			Alkali Metals (Primary Flux)		Alkaline Earths (Secondary Flux)
	SiO$_2$	Al$_2$O$_3$	Na$_2$O	K$_2$O	CaO
UMF	3.70	0.39	0.09	0.18	0.73
Flux Ratio			0.27		0.73

The information that is primarily useful from this exercise is the silica and alumina levels and the flux ratio. Note the fluxes always add up to 1.0.

So now you have your UMF in the bottom row, you might be thinking, what do we do with it? First, it can be plotted out on the Stull Chart; second, we see what the flux ratio looks like; third, it can be used to help substitute materials in the glaze.

Stull Chart
The Stull Chart was created by R.T. Stull in 1912, taking some of the findings of Herman Seger's explorations into the UMF and turning them into a very useful map. It plots the SiO$_2$ (silica) and Al$_2$O$_3$ (alumina) levels of a glaze recipe.

It is useful to plot a recipe on the chart to predetermine whether or not a fired glaze will be glossy, matt, crazed or under-fired. You can treat this as a rough indication, rather than an exact method, as there are variables within firing temperatures and clay bodies to consider.

With this recipe, if we plot the silica levels (3.7) and the alumina levels (0.39) we can see that the glaze is in the glossy, unglazed region – this is for a cone 10 firing. If we wanted to create an even glossier glaze, we could increase the silica levels. If you were to plot the silica and alumina levels of a different glaze, and you find it in the crazed region, you can proportionately alter the silica and alumina levels to get to a non-crazed place on the chart. The appearance of the glaze may change depending on how stringent you are being in retaining the original calculations of the fluxes. In some instances, you may test a glaze to find it crazes, even though it doesn't plot in the crazed region on the chart. This is because all clay bodies differ slightly, so it is good to take this chart as a guide rather than a rule.

Flux Ratio

In order to find out the flux ratio, the alkali metals (primary fluxes or R_2O), which include lithium, sodium and potassium, are added together. Separately, the alkaline earths (secondary fluxes or RO), which include magnesium, calcium, strontium, barium and zinc, are added together. A flux ratio of 0.3 R_2O to 0.7 RO creates the most durable glazes. In this glaze we have 0.27 R_2O to 0.73 RO, which is near enough to the ideal ratio to be suitable. Therefore, before even mixing up and firing this glaze, we can be confident that this looks to be a suitably durable and functional glaze, which we can easily adapt and alter to suit our needs.

Substituting Materials and Altering Glazes

Now that we know how to determine and read the UMF, we also have the knowledge of how to substitute materials. A simple way to do this is to duplicate your UMF table, enter in the material substitution and tweak the proportions until the chemical analysis of both appear the same, or as near as you are able to make it.

For example, to substitute whiting with a wollastonite glaze, consider that whiting is composed of calcium carbonate, while wollastonite is composed of calcium silicate, providing the glaze with both calcium and silica. This is important because it means that a straight swap of materials would definitely alter the chemistry of the glaze, but with the chemical knowledge of the glaze you can establish the required proportion of the substituted material.

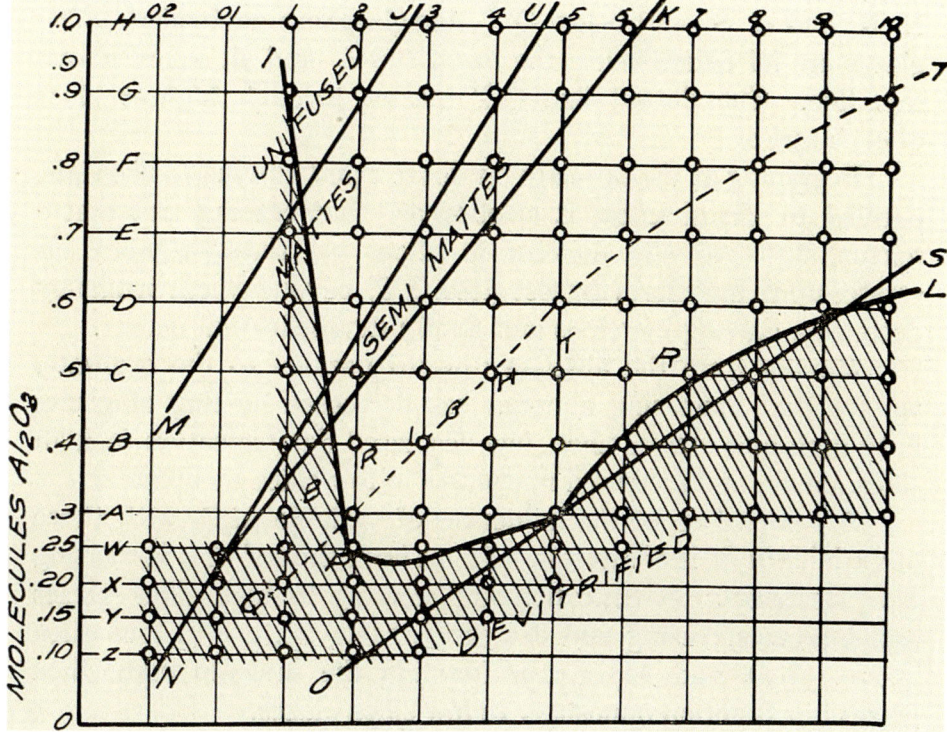

A graph that was created by R.T. Stull in 1912, taking some of the findings of Herman Seger's exploration into the UMF and turning them into a very useful map. It plots the SiO_2 (silica) and Al_2O_3 (alumina) levels of a glaze recipe. It is useful to plot a recipe on the chart to predetermine whether or not a fired glaze will be glossy, matt, crazed or under-fired.

CHAPTER 7

FIRING YOUR WORK

Firing is undoubtedly one of the most exciting aspects of the making process. It is at this point that your wares transform from fragile clay forms into finished, functional ceramic pieces. No matter how many times you've fired a kiln, or how reliable your firing process is, the anticipatory feeling of opening the kiln after a glaze firing never goes away.

Although much of the firing process happens behind closed kiln doors, it is vital to understand the processes taking place within a firing, especially when producing functional tableware. Potters occasionally refer to the firing process as 'magic' or call upon the 'kiln gods' for help, and although we too often use these terms anecdotally, it is important to acknowledge that this is a technical, scientific process within which we are not leaving anything to chance. The firing process is a daunting prospect for many potters at the beginning, but I find it helpful to break the information down into more digestible pieces and it soon feels more accessible.

You will quickly learn that firing techniques and schedules can become highly personal and differ from potter to potter, so it is advisable to keep charts, logs and notes so that you can compare notes between firings.

COMPOSITIONAL CHANGES TO THE CLAY

In order to better understand what is happening to our wares within the firing process, we need to understand about the process of vitrification. Put simply, vitrification is the process of changing the composition of clay with the application of heat and time in order to create a surface impervious to water.

Let's explore exactly what these changes are. Clay is composed of alternating layers of alumina, silica and water. Clay is such an appealing material due to its plastic quality, meaning that it can be easily shaped at the wheel. In order for clay to be plastic it needs to be wet, but being in this wet condition means that, while easy to shape and sculpt, its form is temporary and vulnerable to breakage. Therefore a fundamental transformation needs to take place in order for the pot to become stronger and more permanent, and this has to do with water content.

When clay dries at room temperature, it becomes rigid in form yet extremely fragile. At this point we can still recycle the clay to use again simply by adding water. Pots at this stage of the process are often referred to as 'greenware'. At this point, even though the clay may feel dry to touch, it still contains chemically bound water within its structure.

Wares need to dry completely at room temperature before being fired. This is because any water escaping from the clay as steam could cause it to explode in the kiln. How long a drying time is depends on many factors, such as climate, the time of the year, thickness and the size and shape of the piece. Like many things with pottery, there is not a textbook answer and you are called upon to use your judgement. A general rule of thumb is that if a piece of greenware feels unexpectedly cold to the touch or dark in colour then it

A fully loaded kiln with greenware pots, soon to be biscuit fired. Wares are stacked neatly and are able to touch in the biscuit firing.

is not yet fully dried. You must not rush this stage; however, if you do find yourself in a tight spot for time, a process called 'candling' is a very helpful technique. This involves pre-heating the pots inside the kiln up to 80°C (176°F) for a number of hours before beginning the biscuit firing.

Once the wares are dry, they can be loaded in to the kiln. Up until 100°C (212°F) the remaining 'free' water is evaporating. Dehydroxylation is the name of the process of chemically combined water being driven off and this occurs up to 550°C (1022°F).

From 700–900°C (1292–1652°F), the organic matter within the clay is burned away in the form of carbon dioxide. It is at this point that the clay particles start to bind together and begin to vitrify. A non-reversible change has occurred and at this point the clay cannot be rehydrated and reworked. There has been some shrinkage from the greenware stage and the clay has also changed colour. With some exceptions, your ware is not yet durable enough to use and is not yet fully vitrified, but it is strong enough to handle carefully for the glazing process. The chemical composition of the clay when biscuit fired is $Al_2SO_3 2SiO_2$.

From 900°C (1652°F) onwards, the changes taking place within the structure of the clay are quite complex and depend on the type of clay being used. As stoneware and porcelain are the most common and likely bodies for producing thrown tableware, we will detail these. Above 900°C (1652°F), vitrification begins to take place. The silica within the clay begins to melt. Note that silica has a melting point of 1710°C (3110°F). However, the beginning of the melt, put simply, means that the voids between the clay particles are filled and fuse together, enabling the vessel to become vitrified and functional. At 1000°C (1832°F) the crystals within the clay begin to melt and new crystals, which give the body strength, are formed in their place.

Firing stages of a teapot, from greenware, to biscuit fired to glaze fired.

BISCUIT WARE

There is some discussion as to the name 'biscuit' ware. It is often cited that the word is derived from the Latin *bis* (twice) and *coctus* (cooked), while some think that it may refer to the biscuit-fired surface literally resembling the surface or toasty colour of a biscuit. Perhaps it is both, but often in the UK we use the term 'biscuit' whereas in the US and elsewhere it is often 'bisque'. Both are correct but we will use the term 'biscuit'.

The biscuit firing takes the ware from being in its plastic state to a state in which it is durable enough to handle and porous enough to glaze. We liken a biscuit-ware piece to a sponge – once you dip the ware in the glaze, the water from the glaze is soaked up into the walls of the pot, evaporating over time and leaving a powder coating of glaze upon the surface. Although the biscuit-fired pot feels relatively strong to the touch, it is still fragile and certainly still too porous to be functional.

Most potters producing wheel-thrown tableware take their work through a biscuit firing first of up to about 1000°C (1832°F), depending on the clay body, followed by a glaze firing.

A trolley of biscuit-fired coffee pour-overs. The stoneware used is quite pink at this stage but will change colour again in the glaze firing.

SINGLE FIRING

While it is common practice to follow the system of biscuit firing followed by glaze firing, it isn't essential. Biscuit firing was introduced in or around the seventeenth century as processes became more industrialised, so if we consider pottery to be an ancient and primitive craft, biscuit firing is a relatively new process. Before this, potters would have used clay slip decoration, or simply brushed on dry glazes (which often contained lead and were detrimental to the health of the glazers). It is also possible to raw glaze a greenware pot and fire the piece just the once, which is known as single firing. There are pros and cons to this process. Single firing skips a whole kiln cycle and therefore saves precious energy and the time and labour of loading and unloading kilns. Raw glazing is, however, quite a specialised skill and requires a little more care and attention as the greenware pot is very fragile to hold and the glaze composition needs to be a different formula for the glaze to adhere well.

EARTHENWARE

Some wares can mature within the same temperature range as biscuit ware, including earthenware. Interestingly, with earthenware, the body of the pot remains porous even when fired and it is the glaze that is the vitrified element. It is entirely possible to produce functional tableware from earthenware but it is also worth considering that the clay body is not as strong as high-fired stoneware and porcelain and is more prone to chipping. Furthermore, there is a greater emphasis on the durability of the glaze required.

STONEWARE AND PORCELAIN

Stoneware and porcelain clays demand a higher temperature for maturity, in the region of 1200–1300°C (2192–2372°F).

Stoneware bodies are often grey (unfired) and can contain grog, which is a refractory material either added to the clay in large particles or as fine particles. The grog is added in order to help support the structure of the clay when throwing. Porcelain is usually white in colour and has a delicate materiality and no grog. It is undoubtedly more difficult to work with than stoneware but many potters endure the difficulties as it is such a unique and special material.

PRACTICAL TIPS ON LOADING A KILN

Whether you are loading the kiln for a biscuit firing or for a glaze firing, there are many shared best practices and a few differences to note.

Once you fire in your kiln a few times you'll get to know if there are any cool or hot spots you need to pay attention to, and load the kiln accordingly.

Loading a kiln can feel a bit like trying to solve a puzzle and it is not unusual to need to unload and start again. Try to leave sufficient time for loading the kiln – it takes a lot longer than you might first anticipate but it can be an extremely satisfying and mindful task. Take care during this process, organising your wares with consideration, maximising the space efficiency while you're at it.

Loading a Biscuit Firing

When handling raw pots at the greenware stage, it is important to remember that they are still very fragile and must be handled carefully. Accidents do happen and at least at this point the remnants of your broken greenware can be rehydrated and the clay used again. Always pick up raw pots with support from beneath the pot and never by a handle our spout. Biscuit kilns can be packed tightly with your wares stacked upon or inside another several times. Bowls, mugs, beakers and plates, for example, can be inverted on one another and smaller pots can be placed within larger pots. Care should be taken not to load too much pressure onto shallow open forms or anything delicate in structure. If ever in doubt, it is always a good idea to use a new kiln shelf instead of stacking.

Stacks of greenware pots in the kiln, ready for biscuit firing. Forms such as mugs, bowls and plates can be inverted and stacked. Smaller pieces can nestle in larger pieces too.

TIPS FOR A SUCCESSFUL BISCUIT FIRING

To check if your greenware is dry enough to fire, carefully place the greenware pot to your cheek and if it feels cold, it needs more time to dry before being fired.

Don't be tempted to hurry the drying process – pots need lots of time. If you're in a tight spot, you can candle your wares at a low temperature for a few hours; this should only be attempted on pots that are nearly dry rather than for the whole drying process.

Stack pots on top of one another or inside other pots to make the most of your space. It doesn't matter if the pots are touching one another during a bisque firing but do pay attention to equal weightings so as not to cause any collapsing stacks of pots or warpage.

Leave the bungs out of the bung holes until 500°C (932°F) has been reached or until you are confident that the water evaporation has finished. To find out whether or not the water evaporation has finished, carefully hold a glass over the bung hole: if it clouds up, water is still escaping.

Kiln ventilation is recommended, but if you don't have this, make sure there is a good airflow running through the workspace with open windows. Try to fire when the space isn't been used.

Loading a Glaze Firing

Wares loaded in a glaze-fire loading should not touch one another. This means that pieces cannot be stacked and should sit upon a kiln shelf instead. A useful rule is to ensure that there is a finger's width gap between each pot. It can be useful to use a mirror to check that pieces are not touching when you've loaded the shelf tightly and can't quite see. Bases of pots should be free from glaze because if the glaze touches the shelf it will fuse together.

Sometimes, especially when testing new glazes or being part of communal firings, glaze drips on kiln shelves are inevitable and it is good practice to apply bat wash to the shelves, which lessens the severity of adhesion. As an additional precaution, you may even place risky pots on potter's sand or make clay or refractory discs to catch glaze drips.

While most stoneware pieces are not glazed at the base, sometimes earthenware pieces are because in order for them to be functional and not porous, glaze is required on both sides of the pot. For earthenware pieces of this sort, refractory stilts can be used, which raise the pot from the kiln shelf. Stilts, however, should not be used for stoneware or porcelain firings because the bodies move to a greater degree in the firing and are also more prone to warpage.

When firing something flat covering a large surface area, such as plates, it is crucial to make sure you are not placing

We make refractory wadding discs with the following recipe: two parts fine molochite, two parts alumina, two parts flour and one part china clay, mixing in only enough water to bind everything together. Ensure all the raw materials are combined thoroughly before adding the water. Dry these out – they can be reused multiple times.

A loaded kiln ready to glaze fire. Wares should not touch one another in a glaze firing – aim to leave a finger's width between each pot.

TIPS FOR A SUCCESSFUL GLAZE FIRING

Up to 300°C (572°F), open the spy hole to allow fumes to escape as they can diminish the lifetime of electric kiln elements.

Above temperatures of 300°C (572°F), the bungs should be in the bung holes and the spy holes should be sealed.

The wares should have clean bases so that any traces of glaze don't stick to the kiln shelf.

Use a small mirror when loading the kiln to check that no pots are touching one another.

It is advisable to wait until your kiln is reading below 100°C (212°F) to open and unload the kiln.

Try to alternate biscuit firings and kiln firings to give your elements longevity.

You can make refractory kiln 'biscuits' to put under and glaze tests – or glazes you know to be runny – by combining two parts fine molochite, two parts alumina, two parts flour and one part china clay, mixing in only enough water to bind everything together. Ensure all the raw materials are combined thoroughly before adding the water. Use coarse molochite to sprinkle on the discs when shaping so they don't stick to the board. Dry these out – they can be reused multiple times.

them on warped kiln shelves or two separate shelves butted together. Both the shelves and the wares expand and contract during the firing. The contrast in movement between shelf and ware should be considered as it can cause tension and therefore cracks in the ware. Potter's sand can be used underneath the ware to minimise tension.

It is important not to place the kiln shelves too close to the side of the kiln in order to allow airflow to circulate around all the wares evenly.

MEASURING TEMPERATURE

The biggest factor in the success of the firing is the relationship between temperature and time. Most modern electric kilns are equipped with a digital kiln sitter which will control the firing cycle. However, these go by temperature alone and one of the most important measurements you need to consider in your kiln cycle is heatwork. This is best understood by using pyrometric cones. Heatwork is the

On the left are cones 10 and 11 before firing and on the right are the same cones after a glaze firing.

effect of both time *and* temperature. Think of baking a cake: most recipes instruct the temperature and also for how long to bake the cake. For example, having the cake in the oven at 180°C (356°F) but for only five minutes is not going to bake it, but having it in the oven at say, 50°C (122°F) but for ten hours, will slowly dry it out. It is similar for clay and in fact this variable is just another instrument in getting desired effects out of glazes.

I favour a long soak and a controlled cooling in my firings as my glazes are at their best with this, but for some potters this may be an unnecessary step. You'll gradually learn the best variables for your work but it will take some trial-and-error testing.

Pyrometric cones are small pyramids of ceramic material with gradual increments of flux (a melting agent). They are formulated to melt at different temperatures. Most often we use three cones per firing: two guard cones and one true cone. For example, for a cone 10 firing, one would use a cone 9, cone 10 and cone 11. It would be expected that the cone 9 would be flat, the cone 10 would be curved at 90 degrees and the cone 11 would be mildly affected. By using the three cones we can understand how our kiln is firing and monitor cold and hot spots.

In a gas or wood kiln, cones are important for helping you to understand the atmosphere and temperature *while* you're firing, but in an electric kiln, cones will help you learn about the temperature *after* the firing.

FIRING ATMOSPHERES

There are two types of firing atmospheres: oxidation and reduction. Electric kilns are oxidising and a kiln that burns fuel such as wood or gas is usually (but not always) used for reduction.

The principle of reduction is to restrict the oxygen by blocking the airflow, which means that some of the fuel remains unburned. When this partial combustion occurs, carbon monoxide is produced instead of carbon dioxide. Carbon monoxide is an unstable gas and is desperate to become stable (in the form of carbon dioxide). Oxygen is therefore drawn from within the body of the clay and/or glaze in order for the carbon to bond with the oxygen molecules. In oxidation, as there is no restriction of oxygen, this chemical reaction does not need to occur.

Two bowls in the same celadon-type glaze but the top, blue version is fired in reduction and the bottom, yellow version is fired in oxidation.

So why bother with reduction? The main reason is that you can produce colours and finishes not generally available in oxidation. Well-known examples include celadons and copper reds. A celadon glaze in oxidation would likely be a pale yellow colour as opposed to the pale green-blue in reduction. The oxides most affected by reduction are iron and copper.

Reduction firing is a traditional process and the results can be nuanced and complex – within these methods of firing there are often elements of chance, which can make your wares feel more special, and many potters do covet reduction firing over oxidation. However, it is also worth remembering that in an electric kiln, it is you that must do the work to make your wares special and that is, we think, a great challenge. Exciting effects and glazes can be produced in both oxidation and reduction and there is no one correct method of firing. However, when making thrown tableware it is sensible to consider the unique benefits that different kiln types offer and whether or not it is conducive to your design and production.

Electric

Electric kilns are probably the most common and accessible type of kiln for the majority of potters. If you're part of a co-working pottery space or have your own studio set-up with no outdoor space, you're most likely going to be firing in an electric kiln. An electric kiln works by passing an electric current through elements that are composed of coils of nichrome wire. The coils evenly heat the ware to the required temperature. Electric kilns come in two main shapes (top-loader/barrel-shaped or front-loader/box) and many different sizes.

The benefits of electric kilns are many. Most electric kilns will come with a digital programmer and an instruction manual and are very straightforward to use. Indeed, smaller models can simply be plugged into a normal socket, while larger kilns tend to need three-phase power and the expertise of an electrician to install. It is relatively easy to create consistent firings and therefore electric kilns are ideal when producing small batch tableware. Although not providing a reduction atmosphere, you can produce a lot of exciting glaze results. Furthermore, it is possible to use renewable energy to power a kiln if you connect to the right supplier.

The downsides to working with an electric kiln are that you're unable to achieve true traditional reduction glazes such as celadon. It can be harder to achieve the depth of glaze, with all the inherent character of reduction-fired pieces. Furthermore, there is a maintenance and cost aspect as elements will need changing from time to time. This is relatively straightforward and can be done yourself or by an electrician.

Gas

Just as electric kilns come in many shapes and sizes, so do gas kilns. Some are purchased as they stand and many are custom built. Most gas kilns are outdoors, partially under cover or otherwise in well-ventilated studios. Gas kilns work in much the same way as electric kilns except the heat is created by a flame flowing through the kiln, fuelled by gas.

The benefits of using gas firing for your work is that you can create beautiful reduction glazes with plenty of character. Once you know the kiln well (gas kilns often have cool and hot spots) and you've honed down your ideal firing schedule, you should be able to produce relatively consistent results.

The downside to this type of firing is that you are using fossil fuels to fire the kiln. The firing process is labour intensive as you must be present throughout the firing and there is a degree of additional risk to the firing process than in an electric kiln (for example pieces not reducing well or reaching temperature). The gas canisters must be stored securely. When pricing your work, it is pertinent to consider these extra steps, materials and labour costs.

Wood

Wood firing is the most traditional method and it brings with it great pleasure and excitement. Wood kilns are custom built and there are many typologies, from the huge anagama kilns that fire for days, to smaller and faster firing kilns. Here, the source of the heat comes from burning wood.

With wood firing you can expect to create characterful pots with lots of texture and variation – no two pieces are alike. Traditional reduction glazes can be achieved alongside lots of chance encounters from a sweeping flame and wood ash spilling around. Firing production tableware pieces in this way isn't entirely economical but many wood firers tend to use mugs and other domestic items as 'kiln fillers' to fit around larger, decorative and more expensive work. Wood firing is often a communal activity, which brings a new collaborative dimension to the experience. It is a real skill and requires attention, practice and experience – qualities of which are to be coveted.

Wood kilns require outdoor space within which to securely store and dry wood. A large amount of wood is needed per firing and it can be tricky finding a reliable and affordable source of wood. Organisation is needed and more often than not a wood kiln has a team of potters on its roster to share duties. Firings tend to be a lot longer than in other kilns and as we must be present throughout it is a good idea to have a rota. While amazing results can be achieved, wood firing also brings a higher risk of failure as

A loaded but not yet fired wood kiln at The Manor in Sheffield. Wadding is used to attach the kiln props and kiln shelves as the wood ash circulating through the kiln can cause them to fuse together.

it is temperamental. Firing tableware for commissions in a wood kiln runs a high risk of failure and could become very expensive, but we would say that creating functional wares alongside more experimental larger pieces would be a good way to approach the matter.

Soda Firing

Soda firing is an atmospheric firing process in which sodium oxide is sprayed into an already very hot kiln. Here, it vaporises and leaves glossy flashes of colour and texture on the glazes.

KILN MANAGEMENT

Kiln furniture is expensive and so naturally you'll want to take good care of it. Kiln shelves and props are made from high-grade alumina refractories. Even though they are designed to withstand repeat exposure to high temperatures, shelves can warp over time, but there are measures you can take to prolong their lifespan.

Before you use your kiln shelves for the first time, check that they are dry and in good condition with no warpage. It is a good idea to cure them in the kiln before first use anyway, by slowly heating up the kiln to 100°C (212°F) to drive off any water.

Check for cracks by supporting the shelf at its centre (this can be tricky with a large, round shelf) and tapping with a metal tool; if it rings clearly then all is well, but if muted there may be a crack.

It is good practice to coat shelves with bat wash, but there is no need to coat props. Bat wash can be made from a mix of alumina and china clay or ball clay. Alumina has a melting point of 2072°C (3761.6°F), and so is resistant to heat, and the clay simply adds body to the alumina so that you can easily apply it to the shelf. To apply bat wash, simply mix to a double cream consistency and paint a thin layer; leave to dry and then paint a second layer at 90-degree angles to the first layer. Another method is to use a paint sprayer if you have one. This creates a very even distribution over the kiln shelf. There are several bat wash recipes you can use to mix your own or you can buy ready-made mixes. One problem many people find with mixing their own recipes is that it flakes off after a couple of firings. This is because the clay has a shrinkage rate. You can solve this by calcining your clay first (just put some in a biscuit-fired bowl and add to the biscuit firing). However, it is often easier to purchase the ready-mixed formula.

Should you get any glaze drips on your shelf, use a hammer and chisel to get rid of the drips and then brush over the scar with more bat wash. Always wear goggles and gloves, as the glaze drips will be extremely sharp.

A good tip for preventing warpage of kiln shelves is to rotate them with each firing. You can even mark one side with iron oxide, for example, to help you identify the sides.

There will (usually) be multiple kiln shelves in a firing and kiln props should be vertically stacked in line with one another. It's really important to align these as much as possible to prevent the shelves from warping. Occasionally, if we have a pot with an awkward shape, it may be necessary to break the vertical alignment of the props. Only do this on the top shelf of the kiln stack as the weight load won't make as significant an impact.

The other piece of equipment to pay attention to is the thermocouple. This measures the temperature of the kiln. It is very fragile and could be easily broken if knocked, but also over time it will deteriorate and gradually the temperature reading will become inaccurate.

Painting bat wash onto new kiln shelves. Bat wash is made from refractory materials so that it doesn't melt, and provides a protective coating for the kiln shelves. To apply bat wash simply mix to a double cream consistency and paint a thin layer, leave to dry and then paint a second layer at 90° angles to the first layer.

CHAPTER 8

EXPERIMENTATION AND CREATING MEANING

In previous chapters we've focused on best practices, rules and systems to follow in order to create functional and durable tableware at the wheel. This chapter examines ways in which we can push the functional boundaries a little further, exploring processes and looking at work by other potters who do this to great effect.

We are fortunate that our craft is multi-faceted; we create three-dimensional objects that are both functional and aesthetic but that can also hold meaning through subtle design decisions. As with many craft disciplines, there can come a point at which rules are there to be pushed and occasionally broken in order to innovate and create the unexpected. A parallel can be found between the disciplines of pottery and cooking. The culinary world has embraced this experimental nature over recent years, with a huge focus on innovation in Michelin-starred restaurants – places where food is not just fuel but art – and so too can ceramic tableware be so much more than pure function.

MATERIAL EXPLORATION

As potters, the materials we work with are to be found beneath our feet – deep in the earth and from land and sea vegetation. It can be interesting to foster a more direct connection, incorporating this into tableware design by using foraged raw materials.

Prior to industrialisation and globalisation, most potters would have worked in this way, using whatever clay was to hand and glazing with other available materials. However, most of us now purchase our raw materials as by-products of other, larger industries. It is very easy for us to lose the knowledge of where our materials come from.

A potter needs to possess so many strands of knowledge and skill, from the technical knowledge required for the design and making, to an awareness of geology and chemistry. However, it is also important to respect and be in awe of the natural world, because each time we make a pot we are consuming precious raw materials. Just as with food production, an emphasis on provenance, quality and innovation needs to placed.

Wild Clay

Clay is a universal material and its qualities change depending on its geography. In the UK there is clay of all different types in abundance. Where we live in Yorkshire, the clay is red earthenware, full of iron, and needs a lot of additional raw materials in order to throw with it (although it has been used for centuries in the brick and pipe making industries).

If you are working on a project and designing tableware for a particular context, one way of creating meaning automatically is to incorporate clay from the locality into the design. This doesn't necessarily need to be the clay body – clay can be used in glazes and slips to great effect. A slip is simply clay combined with water; it is what we use as a type of 'glue' when adding handles or spouts, for example. However, it can also be used as a layer applied onto greenware and over-glazed. Ceramicist Luna van Mierlo experiments

Close-up image of a beaker thrown using an oyster shell as a rib tool and glazed in a glaze recipe using calcined oyster shells as an ingredient.

with foraged clays by using them as slips applied directly to greenware. She applies delicate brushwork using latex, which then peels off to reveal layers of slip, exposed clay and glaze. It is an exciting way of adding texture, colour and meaning to a pot.

Another way to experiment with slip as a decorative tool is through the reductive process of sgraffito. In this method, one or two layers of glaze or slip are applied and then patterns, words or motifs are scratched off to reveal a contrasting colour.

If you would like to use foraged clay for throwing you will need to process it first, as when freshly dug it will be contaminated with substances other than clay. Processing wild clay is a rewarding and enlightening experience. There are a few 'rules' to follow when foraging.

First, be sure to obtain permission from the landowner and observe any laws that may restrict you from taking clay. Never dig in spiritual or religious sites without the owner's permission.

Second, be gentle. Remember that the soil in which you are digging is alive and home to lots of creatures and ecosystems, and although it seems strong, is quite fragile. Clay can often be found in abundance near rivers and coastlines due to the powerful movement of water, which over many years breaks down the rock particles and eventually transforms into clay. These places are often the best place to look. Don't take clay from an eroding cliff edge. While there is often clay found in a location like this, first, it can be dangerous, and second, you may be, even in a small way, contributing to the erosion.

Never take more clay than you need. Instead, make a note of the place. Try to find out as much as you can about the area, its history, its cultural context and so on. Reflect on the connection you feel with the place rather than solely using it as a resource. It is not a novelty and with the act of foraging for raw materials comes a certain responsibility.

How to Process Wild Clay

The process of transforming the earth into workable clay is relatively simple, if not laborious. If you are using clay that has been gathered previously and is relatively dry, you must rehydrate it. Break up the large pieces of earth into smaller segments in a big tub – a plasterer's bath is ideal – using a sledgehammer. Then with your hands, make the particles as small as possible. Water is then added and left to slake.

The next process is to sieve the clay. Begin with a regular soil sieve to remove any stones and then a finer mesh sieve.

Three tests by Luna van Mierlo using layers of slip and glaze, using samples of clay collected from three locations on a Norfolk beach.

Removing excess water from the top of slaked clay, in a plasterer's bath. The yellow colour of this foraged clay is due to the high amounts of iron in the earth.

This is quite a slow process. Once sieved, the clay is left to dry on plaster bats or in old pillowcases strung up to drip dry.

Once it has dried a little, wedge the clay and then it is ready to use. The first thing to do with your processed clay is make a little pinch pot to see how plastic it is – if there are lots of cracks it means it is not very plastic. Also place the small pinch pot on an old biscuit-fired piece and fire it to see how it melts. Has it slumped? Has it melted? What is the shrinkage rate? You will likely need to establish a new temperature to fire to. You may find the shrinkage rate is quite extreme or that it doesn't have much plasticity to it. Just as in the commercial clays we purchase, it is very common and easy to add other raw materials such as fireclay or sand (this helps reduce shrinkage rates) or ball clay (this increases plasticity). Just as with everything else in pottery, this is a trial-and-error process with no defined rules; you must go ahead and experiment on your own to create the clay that works best for you.

Ash

Ash from plants can be incorporated into glazes and this is such an exciting concept. Plants absorb minerals from the earth and as a result are rich in many of the substances we use in our glazes, such as silica, alumina, calcium, potassium, phosphorous, magnesium and iron. An extremely simple glaze can be made by combining clay (alumina) with wood ash (silica and flux). It is so exciting to use a substance that is specific to the geology in which it has grown and therefore meaning is automatically created through this act. One of the big problems however is that the chemical composition of foraged plants and their ashes is so variable, even within the same plant, and so maintaining consistency and repeatability is difficult. We have to embrace this unpredictability when working with ashes (unless you obtain a chemical analysis each time you process ash!).

Processing Ash

Processing ash for glazes is quite simple. First you must collect, dry and burn the material. The same rules of foraging for clay apply to foraging for plants and rocks. If you would like to repeat the glaze in future, take a note of the date of collection and location. Many people use ash from their log burner but if not you can burn the material outside on a clear, windless day. It is important that it isn't too windy as you don't want the fine particles you are trying to collect to be blown away or the plant to become wet from the rain. Be wary of using an old bin or incinerator, as the ash will likely become contaminated with iron from the rust. I have seen people use an old drum of a washing machine or simply a metal pan or tray held over a gas flame.

Once you have the ash ready and cooled (always cover if storing outside), sieve it first through a regular sieve to remove any lumps of charcoal or other objects. Be sure to wear gloves, eye protection and a mask as it will be quite dusty and ash is a very caustic material.

You need to decide whether or not to wash your ash. The advantages of washing the ash is that you are removing the soluble alkaline and caustic materials from the ash, which irritate the skin. Some potters think that unwashed ash can cause problems with the melt but in our experience it isn't so, only that it can cause less consistent results, as unwashed ash retains trace alkaline materials that would normally be washed away in the washing process. We do find however that some of the fluxing properties are reduced in washed ash. It comes down to a personal preference, but because we always aim for consistency and precision, and we want to reduce the skin irritation that comes with unwashed ash, we like to wash our ash. It does make it a lengthier process though and you may find it an unnecessary step, especially if you are looking for very high flux and 'wild' glazes – follow your instinct.

If not washing the ash, you can choose either to store the ash dry or in water. Wood ash often contains debris so we would suggest sieving even just through a garden sieve, either wet or dry. If adding water, do not add too much – just enough to make it damp – and be sure not to discard any of the water as this contains the alkaline materials you are hoping to preserve. Continue to wear a mask, gloves and eye protection and sieve in at least an 80 mesh sieve then store. Do be very careful when handling it or using it when glazing as it will irritate your skin, causing a rash and sometimes bleeding.

If washing, simply submerge the loosely sieved ash in water for at least a couple of days. You'll notice a yellowish soapy substance at the top of the bucket. This is lye and is a very alkaline substance traditionally used in soap making – this is the irritant mentioned previously. Remove this from the top of the bucket and then soak again, and again until the water is much clearer. I repeat the process about two or three times over a week. Next, still wearing protective equipment, sieve the ash through 80 and 100 mesh sieves (if a fine mesh size is desired – again, it is personal preference). Then lay the washed ash out in old biscuit-ware plates or plaster bats to dry or keep as wet ash. Once dry it will be ready to use and, although gloves should still be worn, it should no longer irritate your skin.

Ash can be used as a raw material in your glazes or sprinkled over the top of a freshly glazed ware. Some potters even apply glue to a pot and roll it in ash.

Wood and Plant Ash

Wood ash is often used to create traditional-looking surfaces with rich green hues and often some interesting speckling and variation. It is most often used in reduction but it can be used in oxidation also. If wood firing, the ash from the fuel moves around the kiln chamber and often affects glazes in an atmospheric way. Rice husk is famously used in traditional chun and nuka glazes, and has an opalescent blue. In the UK, rice isn't grown but an alternative could be grasses, straw and reeds.

Seaweed

Seaweed has been used for centuries in ceramics and glass industries as it is readily available and very high in flux, depending on the variety used. It can be processed in the same way as other plant ashes or some potters simply wrap pots in seaweed and fire. One thing to be aware of with seaweed is that it does contain arsenic in small quantities and, if burning for ash, or using seaweed ash in the kiln, care should be taken to ventilate the kiln and the space – this is for both your own health and safety and so as not to ruin your kiln. Seaweed ash can also contain high levels of water-soluble salts that may contaminate the kiln if a great quantity is used, and also cause problems with the clay and glaze, bloating or crawling. Washing the ash should reduce this a little. Care and experimentation are needed.

Shells and Other Sources of Calcium

Shells can be exciting to use in glazes or, more commonly, as wadding for pots. Shells are a source of the flux calcium.

To use in a glaze, the shells need to be fired in a biscuit cycle (to calcine them), then crushed to a powder ready to use and then used in place of whiting. However, I have found that there are some shrinkage problems with using shells in place of whiting and my glazes have often crawled. I often use shells as wadding, placing a pot atop clay-filled shells. The shells turn to pure calcium, which, when soaked in water after firing, dissolve, leaving only a beautiful trace upon the glaze. Plus, the salt within the shell can volatise, causing beautiful orange flashes to the exposed clay. Be aware when using shells, particularly oyster shells, as they are a bit like filters and may contain more trace minerals and chemicals than you hoped (including lead). Eggshells and bones could also be used as a source of calcium and can be processed in the same way as shells for use in glazes.

Artist and potter Chloé Rosetta Bell often uses foraged site-specific materials in her work. A research project that started in 2019 – a collaboration with Halen Môn, who produce sea salt – culminated in a collection of bowls and vases made from seaweed and mussel shells found at the beach at Halen Môn, alongside the chalk residue from the process of washing the sea salt.

Oyster shells in the kiln – these are biscuit fired to 'calcine' them.

Once calcined, the oyster shells are crushed to a powder using a pestle and mortar.

Chapter 8 – Experimentation and Creating Meaning

The ridges on this beaker form (glazed but unfired) were created using an oyster shell as a throwing tool, and the glaze includes oyster shell in place of whiting.

The finished, fired, beaker. Fired in reduction, the blue colour is due to 1 per cent added iron oxide and also the naturally occurring iron within the shell.

A vase by Chloé Rosetta Bell created as part of the research project with Halen Môn.

Detailed view of the vase by Chloé Rosetta Bell, including residue of where the vase has been in contact with shells during the firing.

Rocks

The majority of the raw materials we use in glazes are derived from rocks and so it makes sense that you can experiment with foraging for rocks and earth and using them in your glazes. We would recommend reading a basic geology book to become better equipped with the knowledge of different types of rock.

Fine particles of rocks can often be found on the edges of waterways and lakes. These are either from rocks nearby or perhaps have travelled with the water courses over many years. Another good place to look is on beaches.

Feldspar is a mineral that can either be found as a rock or combined with other substances in a rock. Granite, for example, is formed of feldspar, silica and mica. Feldspars and granites are quite abundant but they aren't always easy to identify – they are usually pink or white and found in the seams of other rocks.

Silica is abundant in most rocks. Quartz and flint pebbles are the purest forms and sandstone is silica sand (quartz broken down and re-formed into a rock). Sand from the beach is a source of silica but will also contain fragments of other rocks too.

Iron ochre is another very abundant material and is a rust-coloured pigment that is often easy to spot in rivers and slow-moving waterways.

Processing Rocks

Hard rocks will need to be heated first, in a biscuit firing, so that you are able to crush them into a powder. Please note that sometimes rocks explode in the kiln! The best way to heat the rocks is to conceal them with spare kiln bricks so that if they do shatter they will not damage the kiln. Also be sure to vent the kiln and space adequately. After heating in this way, a hard rock should be easy to break up and grind in a pestle and mortar. After this it can be sieved to the desired mesh size and then it is ready for experimentation.

EXPLORING FORM

While there are many rules to follow in order to produce a well-crafted and durable piece of tableware made at the wheel, there are also rules to be broken in order to create

A porcelain plate fired in oxidation in a rutile and iron glaze as part of Pottery West's 'Wilder' project. The plate was thrown onto three stilt-like feet, which caused it to distort and slump in the firing.

Plate by Janaki Larsen. Larsen is often playful with form and glaze, pushing the boundaries of functionality to their limits to create meaning, poetry and beauty.

something more akin to art, or at least, innovation: plates that are distorted or cracked; glazes that crawl and craze; bowls that wobble. Breaking the convention elevates ideas and plays with expression and meaning. Plus, they tap into something that nature does so well, a fine balance between order and disorder, function of dysfunction. Creating pieces like this may not do for an everyday domestic setting, but for a special dining experience or concept it could do.

Once you have an understanding of how your materials work, you can play with them in this way. Some years ago we produced a limited edition of porcelain plates, each one trimmed onto three stilt-like 'feet' that, when fired, caused the porcelain to warp and slump in sculptural ways.

Canadian artist and potter Janaki Larsen has produced tableware for some of the most renowned restaurants in the world; her distinctive style plays with the boundaries of what is functional to maximum effect, with plates seemingly fraying at the edges or having cracks, and glazes showing the drama and spectacle of the firings in which they were created.

Form can also be explored in a more technical manner, producing more complex or ambitiously scaled pieces with multiple components that must fit together to create something almost sculptural, yet not always entirely practical.

Cooking and food can be a spectacle, something theatrical, and so the tableware used to serve it should play a role as well.

Plates and bowls by Pottery West in an assortment of glazes and clay bodies.

CHAPTER 9

CREATING A STUDIO LAYOUT FOR HAND-THROWN TABLEWARE PRODUCTION

A pottery studio specialising in the production of hand-thrown tableware requires specific tools and space-planning best practices. Many potters, particularly those working out of home studios and garages, may not have ample space to play with, but there is still a great deal we can do to optimise a space. This chapter aims to provide some best practices and a comprehensive list of tools to acquire, plus some health and safety considerations that all potters should educate themselves with.

SPACE PLANNING

In our experience, if there is one thing a potter is adept at, it is organising and fitting a lot of equipment and materials into a less than ideally proportioned space. A pottery studio has to perform an array of functions and many potters are working with a smaller than desired footprint. There are certain items of equipment and material storage that take up a lot of floorspace and there are also considerations of cleanliness, in particular, dust, to contend with. When producing hand-thrown tableware, there is an extra space burden we must consider, and that is the fact that we make in batches rather than single wares. Extra space is required to dry and store pots in progress.

Something less practical, but in our opinion very important, is to think about how your studio space makes you feel. After all, this is a space within which you will spend many hours, some of this time in a creative state, requiring inspiration and a clear head. I always strive for a studio space that has some order to it, lots of natural light and special shelves onto which I can place pieces, inspiration, books and ideas.

One final piece of advice is to have as much equipment and furniture on wheels as possible (even our kiln has wheels). This ensures we can easily move heavy materials and equipment for use and also to clean underneath where dust gathers.

Matt working at the wheel in our busy production studio. (Photo: India Hobson)

Inside Carla Murdoch's home studio, which is in a converted garage. Carla makes the most out of a small space with under-counter storage and shelves.

1. Throwing and Trimming Space

A great deal of time will be spent at the wheel so choose a space that has natural light and is uplifting in some way. If possible, organise your ware board shelving to be in front of your wheel rather than to the side so that you are not twisting to lift pieces from the wheel and onto a shelf.

If you are working with both stoneware and porcelain, it is a good idea to have two separate wheels to avoid cross-contamination. Admittedly this is a luxury that not many potters can indulge in, so if not, ensure that you clean the wheels and tools very thoroughly before changing your clays.

Some potters position their wheels on a table and throw in a standing position as this lessens the risk of back pain.

The wheel is positioned with trolleys on wheels nearby, an ergonomic stool and a mirror.

2. Fettling Space

Fettling clay at greenware stage and also sanding biscuit ware before glazing creates a lot of airborne dust that is very harmful to our lungs. Over time, the silica in this dust fills the lungs and causes silicosis or cancer. Always wear a mask when fettling or sanding. Measures can also be made to lessen the severity of dust production, such as wet sanding, using a dust extraction system and never sweeping a floor – only mopping or wet hoovering.

3. Water and Clay Trap

A source of water is important. If you don't have a tap and sink plumbed in your studio, you'll need a water storage option because you'll need water for throwing, cleaning, glazing and so on.

A clay trap is a good idea. This is a storage container fitted below your sink within which the clay and glaze debris sinks down and separates from the waste water. This means pipes won't become clogged with clay and that hazardous

A dedicated glazing space and raw material storage is useful. We keep large bags of raw materials stowed away on dollies beneath counters and decant into plastic boxes for ease of use.

materials don't enter the water system. It does need to be cleaned on a regular (if possible weekly) basis. You can create a low-budget option by just leaving waste throwing water in a bucket and siphoning off the water from the top, as the clay will have sunk to the bottom. Use plaster bowls to speed up the process and then either discard the slurry or find a way to reuse the waste material.

In winter, it can be a cold pursuit to sit at a wheel with your hands in water, throwing. Try to use warm water if possible for a more pleasant experience. When producing thrown tableware in batches, it can be a long time spent at the wheel so it is a good idea to look after the basics.

4. Pug Mill and Reclaim Area

A pug mill is a heavy-use piece of machinery that mixes clay. It is a relatively expensive piece of equipment and not essential. Without a pug mill, clay must simply be wedged by hand before throwing.

A pug mill is particularly useful for the reclaim process and saves an enormous amount of time and labour from wedging and reclaiming all the clay that needs recycling from throwing and trimming sessions.

Plaster bats are useful, if not essential, for drying the reclaimed clay on. The plaster absorbs the moisture of the clay so that after a while it is ready to be wedged and reused.

5. Kiln Space

The kiln is an essential piece of equipment for your studio and will require not only the space for the kiln but a space of approximately 50cm (20in) around it too. This needs to be a well-ventilated area either near a window or with added extraction. Gas kilns are often built in covered outdoor spaces though not always. Special requirements are needed to ensure the safety of using a gas kiln indoors, such as plenty of ventilation and a secure storage facility for the gas.

The kiln space also needs a place to store the kiln furniture. Kiln shelves should be stored upright in a dry area. It is useful to have space to store props so that you can access them easily when loading the kiln. We talked in further detail about the firing process in Chapter 7.

6. Glazing Area

As glaze buckets are heavy, it is a good idea to store them also on dollies so they can be moved around the space as necessary. Similar to the fettling space, good management of dust and cleanliness is important in the glazing area. Having plenty of surface space is helpful when glazing tableware.

OTHER USEFUL SPACE ORGANISING TIPS

Dedicated Storage Spaces

The wares you produce will have plenty of downtime in between the various stages of throwing, trimming, fettling, firing, glazing and so on. In fact, a great deal of the space required in the studio is for storing work in progress and should you fail to factor this into your space design, the studio will quickly descend into chaos. Furthermore, storage for raw materials, packaging, finished work and miscellaneous equipment, such as tools and kiln equipment, should be considered.

Clay

Fortunately, clay doesn't have a shelf life. Indeed, some potters consider that the older the clay is the better, often prizing clay that has formed mould to be of better quality for making pots with! Over time you may find the clay stored in bags dries out, which is merely an inconvenience. Dried-out clay can be rehydrated and reworked with some attention. Storage of your clay should be in an easy-to-access space where you don't have to twist and lift. Again, many potters are not working in designed-to-purpose buildings and it is not uncommon to have to lift tonnes of clay up flights of stairs with each delivery.

Work in Progress

A significant amount of time in the work-in-progress lifespan of your wares is spent simply sitting on a shelf drying. All studios offer different conditions but for any outdoor studio spaces such as garages, watch out for cold weather. Freezing temperatures cause the water in the drying clay to freeze and contract and the piece will be ruined. Alternatively, spaces that are too hot are prone to drying too quickly and also cracking. People make pots all over the world in varying conditions and we potters are very resourceful people. In the UK, we experience extremely varied weather conditions from week to week and so we are often responding to our conditions and weather. Big sheets of plastic that can be purchased, or even better recycled from something else, are so useful for covering wares to prevent them drying out too quickly. If you need to leave a larger than optimum time between throwing and trimming, cover with plastic, seal and spritz with water using a spray bottle. Some potters in damp conditions use a dehumidifier to speed up the process. With time you'll get to know what you need to do.

Raw Materials

An area to store raw materials for glazing is important. It is cheaper to buy raw materials in bulk if you have the space to store them. Under-cabinet trolleys are useful for storing large sacks of raw materials and then smaller plastic containers with well-fitting lids can be used for decanting smaller amounts into.

Packaging

A larger than often anticipated space is needed to store packaging materials, especially if you are planning on selling your tableware to customers. If possible, this should be a clean, dry and dust-free space. Many potters don't have ample storage space but the more space you can allocate to packaging materials the better, as purchasing in bulk keeps the prices down.

A place to keep finished wares is a great idea if you have space in the studio.

Finished Wares

In each of our studios this is a storage space we have always failed to prioritise but if you have the space, having a special home for finished pieces is so rewarding. After all the hard work you've put in, it's great to see the fruits of your labour proudly displayed. On a less positive note, we like to have a dedicated space for the pots that haven't gone so well: a place for seconds that we will either sell or give away; a place for pots we would like to keep because they amuse us in their character (albeit defunct!); finally, a pile that we will smash – a last resort.

TIPS FOR STAYING SAFE

Clay dust is full of silica, which can be breathed in easily and over time settles in our lungs. This can cause diseases such as silicosis or even cancer. The good news is that there are many measures we can take to prevent this from happening. Masks made from cloth or basic models of dust mask do not offer enough protection against silica, which is extremely fine and can remain airborne for some time. The best option is a mask with a high dust filtration of P3/P100. Ensure the mask fits well and has no gaps around your nose or mouth area. It can be uncomfortable to wear at first but you'll soon get used to it.

If working with dry wares, for example, fettling or sanding, or else cleaning, measuring glaze powders or indeed anything generating an amount of dust, wear a mask. It is even better if you can install a dust extraction system to the area in which you are generating dust. Where possible, use water in these processes to minimise airborne dust.

Cleanliness is important. Draw up a daily, weekly and monthly cleaning schedule to help get yourself into a good routine. Never ever sweep floors – always wet hoover or mop. Clear up clay and glaze spills before they dry.

When working with glaze, wear protective gloves to prevent skin irritation or even absorption through the skin. Do not have food or drink in the same area that you keep or work with glazes. Keep raw materials in containers with well-fitting lids and clearly label them. Keeping them in containers rather than bags is not only more secure, it is easier to measure from them without generating as much dust. When measuring out glazes, add directly to water to prevent dust generation.

TOOLS AND EQUIPMENT

Building up your studio from scratch is no mean feat. There is a lot of equipment to purchase. The most important items are the wheel and the kiln; the other items can be added as and when. Don't be afraid of using second-hand equipment. Scour eBay and contact art schools (sadly many ceramics departments have or will be closed down and they are often selling or even giving away some great equipment). Potters' groups, magazines and suppliers also list equipment being sold quite frequently.

1. Wheel

Most potters use an electric wheel but kick wheels are also popular. Different brands and models are good for different things. It is unlikely that you'll require a heavy-weight wheel for creating tableware.

A mirror is, in our opinion, an essential tool when working at the wheel as you can better see the progress of your work and if the profile you are working on is right. A self-supporting mirror is ideal.

You can purchase an ergonomic and cushioned throwing stool on which the legs can be adjusted. This is a good idea to help alleviate the back pain that is so common when working at the wheel for long periods of time.

A trolley or shelf for your tools, notes and container for reclaim is a good idea for beside your wheel.

2. Shelving and Ware Boards

Many potters favour free-standing shelving on wheels that can be moved around the space. In our studio we use custom-made trolleys but we've seen many potters use bakery trolleys. If there is no space for this it is possible to use racking on the walls onto which you can place ware boards. One note of caution though is that this can mean that pots dry unevenly, and attention must be made to turn ware boards regularly.

Ware boards are long planks of wood onto which wares can be stored. Untreated Indonesian/Malaysian/Brazilian plywood of 18mm (¾in) thickness is a good suggestion for a relatively resilient wood to use. Over time, they will eventually warp, but are so much more durable than other types of wood. You can buy the wood and get it cut to size at a timber merchants. Don't coat the ware boards with varnish because we want the wood to absorb some of the moisture of the thrown wares to avoid cracks. The dimensions of your ware boards can be custom to your situation but it is a good idea to choose a length and width that will fit a good amount of wares on and still be light enough to lift and move around. For example, the boards we used in our studio measure 30cm × 100cm × 1.8cm (12in × 39in × ¾in).

3. Throwing Bat System

For pieces that you can't take off the wheel head in case of distorting, such as wide-based items like shallow bowls and plates, you'll need throwing bats.

There are different ways and systems of working with bats. You can simply attach a wooden bat to your wheel head using clay but this isn't a great method for producing in batch quantities, as the clay decompresses over the throwing session and, if working with a throwing gauge, it causes the dimensions you are working with to alter.

A better system for repetition throwing is either to drill into your wheel head and attach pins with corresponding holes in the bat, or you can purchase, or have custom-made, a bat system within which only the inner square of the bat is removed and replaced with each piece. This works well for smaller items such as mugs.

4. Pug Mill

A pug mill is not an essential piece of machinery but it is useful. You can purchase a de-airing version that also has a vacuum and removes air from the clay so that it is ready to use.

5. Kiln

Kilns can either be self-built (more common for gas and wood kilns) or purchased. Electric kilns are either top-loaders of front-loaders. It is down to personal preference. I personally favour top-loaders as I find them easier to load. If you are going to be doing a lot of glaze testing, it is really useful to have a small test kiln. Speak to a kiln supplier about your requirements as they are usually extremely helpful.

6. Kiln Furniture

Kiln furniture comes in the form of kiln shelves, props and Orton cones. They can be purchased from most pottery suppliers in all sorts of shapes and sizes. With repeated usage at high temperatures, kiln shelves do have a tendency to warp and need to be replaced. A good tip is to turn the shelves with each firing.

7. Tools

There is no right and wrong way of using pottery tools. It seems to be a very personal thing, with no two potters using the same method. *Refer* back to Chapters 3 (throwing and trimming tools) and 5 (glazing tools) for more detail about the types of tools needed.

Tips for Maintaining Tools

With regular use, tools will wear out and need to be replaced. However, steps can be taken to care for and prolong the lifespan of your tools. Never leave metal tools in water where they will quickly rust. Invest in a tool sharpener; this can be used to sharpen trimming tools, which wear out particularly quickly.

Once every few months we like to wash our brushes in almost boiling soapy water before being rinsed in cold water and left to dry.

Plaster Bats

Plaster is a form of calcium sulphate in its powder form and when water is added it forms into a hardened surface that is really absorbent. It's perfect for using to reclaim clay or other raw materials as it soaks up the excess water quickly. It is quite straightforward to make your own plaster bat. When working with plaster, be very careful not to cross-contaminate the plaster and the clay because if any plaster gets into the clay, your work will be ruined. If possible, mix the plaster in a separate space, and remember that plaster sets quickly so you'll need to be organised and work quickly.

First you will need to work out the plaster-to-water ratio. Work out the volume of the bat by measuring the length, height and width. The plaster you use will have instructions for the best consistency to use, but it is usually about 70 (which means 70 parts water to 100 parts plaster).

This is an accurate formula to use:

Volume in cubic cm × 0.6 = x grams of water

Grams of water × (100 ÷ 70) = x grams of potter's plaster

To make a plaster bat, you'll need a sheet of glass or Perspex and four cottle boards (or anything that can be used as a forma). Use clamps to keep your boards in place. You'll also need gloves and a mask. Cover any clay work in progress and try to keep plaster contamination as minimal as possible.

You can seal the edges of the boards with clay, though it isn't always essential.

With clean water at room temperature in a bowl or bucket, start adding handfuls of plaster evenly and quickly over the surface of the water by letting it sift through your fingers. Slake the plaster until the plaster is absorbed by the water. Do not be tempted to mix; just let the water absorb into the plaster.

Using your hands, mix the plaster until there are no lumps left and the plaster begins to thicken (this takes approximately three minutes but this can vary depending on the brand of plaster).

Tap the bucket quickly to bring up any air bubbles and then pour steadily into the mould and leave to set. Use a piece of wood to break the fall of the plaster to prevent air bubbles emerging.

Once the plaster is set, remove the cottle boards. The plaster may still be warm. You can use a rasp to soften the edges of the plaster so that they are less prone to chipping with use. Leave it to dry thoroughly before its first use. Clean everything thoroughly to prevent contamination.

Teapot, pourer and egg cup. (Photo: India Hobson)

SELECTED GLAZE RECIPES AND FORMULAS

GLAZE RECIPES

Charcoal, Cone 10, Oxidation
Potassium feldspar 39
Whiting 19
Kaolin Grolleg 24
Flint 4
Calcium borate frit 4

Colourants
Red iron oxide 4
Cobalt carbonate 2
Nickel oxide 4

Shino, Cone 10, Reduction – Special Effect Glaze
Sodium feldspar 30
Hyplas ball clay 25
Spodumene 25
Nepheline syenite 8
Soda ash 7
Kaolin Grolleg 5

Detail image of our 'charcoal' glaze. (Photo: India Hobson)

A cup in our shino-type glaze. This glaze, fired in reduction, is whiter when applied thickly and more orange when thin. It also has pleasing black and metallic spots from carbon trapping.

Speckled White, Cone 10, Oxidation

Potash feldspar 36
Whiting 7
Dolomite 6
Talc 7
Flint 17
Calcium borate frit
or colemanite 3
Kaolin Grolleg 23

Colourants
Tin oxide 8

USEFUL FORMULAS

Specific Gravity
To work our specific gravity (SG), divide the weight in grams of substance by the amount in millilitres.

Water-to-Plaster Ratio for Making Plaster Bats
Volume in cubic cm × 0.6 = x grams of water
Grams of water × (100 ÷ 70) = x grams of potter's plaster

Various forms thrown in a flecked stoneware and glazed in our 'speckled white' glaze. This glaze is the base for most of our own glazes, which then use different oxides to produce varying colours. (Photo: India Hobson)

CONTRIBUTORS AND SUPPLIERS

CONTRIBUTORS

Carla Murdoch Ceramics
www.carlamurdochceramics.co.uk
Photographer credit: Carla Murdoch

Chloé Rosetta Bell
www.chloerosettabell.com
Photographer credit: Chloé Rosetta Bell

Janaki Larsen
www.janakilarsen.com
Photographer credit: Janaki Larsen

Kim Lê
www.atelierkimle.com
Photographer credit: Madeleine Froment

Luna van Mierlo
Instagram: @lunavanmierlo_ceramics

Pottery West
www.potterywest.co.uk
Photographer credit: Pottery West, India Hobson

SUPPLIERS

www.bathpotters.co.uk
www.ctmpotterssupplies.co.uk
www.potclays.co.uk
www.potterycrafts.co.uk
www.rs-components.com (for safety equipment)
www.scarva.com
www.valentines.co.uk

BIBLIOGRAPHY AND FURTHER READING

Atkin, J., *250 Tips, Techniques and Trade Secrets for Potters* (Herbert Press, 2009)

Bloomfield, L., *Science for Potters* (The American Ceramic Society, 2017)

Clark, K., *The Potter's Manual: Complete, Practical Essential Reference for All Potters* (Macdonald Orbis, 1987)

Cooper, E., *The Potter's Book of Glaze Recipes* (A&C Black, 2004)

Daly, G., *Developing Glazes* (Herbert Press, 2013)

Forrest, M., *Natural Glazes, Collecting and Making* (Bloomsbury, 2013)

Hamer, F., and Hamer, J., *The Potter's Dictionary of Materials and Techniques* (A&C Black, 1997)

Leach, B., *A Potter's Book* (Faber and Faber, 2011)

Levy, M., Shibata, H., and Shibata, T., *Wild Clay: Creating Ceramics and Glazes from Natural and Found Sources* (Herbert Press, 2022)

Murfitt, S., *The Glaze Book: A Visual Catalogue of Decorative Ceramic Glazes* (Thames & Hudson, 2002)

Rogers, P., *Ash Glazes: Techniques and Glazing from Natural Sources* (Herbert Press, 2023)

Wensley, D., *Pottery: A Manual of Techniques* (The Crowood Press, 1989)

WEBSITES AND COURSES

www.ceramicmaterialsworkshop.com
www.glazy.org

GLOSSARY

Anagama An ancient type of wood-fired kiln, like a tunnel with a series of steps. Often fires for a long duration.

Atom The smallest particle of an element that can exist.

Bat A disc, usually made of wood, for throwing wares on.

Bat wash A coating of refractory materials, usually alumina and china clay, used to protect kiln shelves from glaze drips during firings.

Biscuit/Bisque Clay ware after it has been fired to roughly 1000°C (1832°F) (first firing). It is not yet vitrified but a chemical change has occurred and it is now ceramic; moisture within the clay has been slowly driven off. Biscuit ware is often glazed or decorated before being fired once again.

Blanks (that is, handle blanks) Semi-pulled handles before they are attached to the body of a mug or jug form.

Body A term used to describe a particular mixture of clay, such as a stoneware body or porcelain body.

Calcining The process of heating a substance to a high temperature for the purpose of oxidising or removing volatile substances.

Calliper An instrument used to measure the diameter of an object.

Chamois leather A type of porous leather, usually made from sheepskin. It can be used as a useful tool to smooth rims when throwing or as a base on which to trim wares on.

Chemical reaction When substances combine to make a new substance with different properties, weight and appearance.

Chuck Clay thrown or moulded into a shape to support or hold a ware in place while being trimmed. Usually the chuck is thrown and used when leather hard and then recycled. It can also be biscuit fired and reused.

Clay trap A system for collecting clay and glaze deposits to prevent them draining down the sink and clogging pipes.

Coiling A method of hand-building pots by using coils of clay.

Collaring Squeezing the walls of a ware to shape a neck of part of a form.

Crawling A glaze defect caused by surface tension in the melting glaze that can sometimes be caused by application errors or having too much clay in the glaze and not enough flux.

Crazing A glaze defect, when the fired glaze develops fine racks caused by the contraction of the glaze.

Dehydroxylation The process of chemically combined water being driven off, occurring up to 550°C (1022°F).

Earthenware A clay body fired to a relatively low temperature, often, but not always, red in colour. It remains porous and so requires a glaze if intended for food and drink.

Element A substance that cannot be broken down into other substances. Each chemical element is distinguished (as per the periodic table) by the number of protons in the nuclei of its atoms. This is known as the atomic number.

Eutectic The point at which a mixture of substances melts at a temperature (that is lower than the melting points of the separate constituents).

Fettling The process of cleaning up wares, often with a sponge or knife, at leather-hard stage. It can also apply to the process of smoothing out glazes.

Firing The process of applying heat and time to a ware to bring clay and glaze to maturity.

Firing atmosphere The 'atmosphere' of the kiln, whether oxidation, reduction and so on.

Flange (for example, of a lid) The ridge on a neck of a pot or lid, usually for adding stability.

Flashing Usually occurs on exposed clay surfaces exposed to variations in flame, ash and vapours such as salt.

Flocculation A process of particles clumping and gelling in glaze or slip, which would otherwise be thin and runny.

Flux An ingredient used in a glaze formula that helps the silica and alumina to melt at a lower temperature.

Flux ratio The proportion of primary and secondary flux or $R_2O:RO$.

Formula The chemical analysis of a glaze recipe.

Gallery The part of the neck or shoulder of a pot upon which a lid sits.

Glaze A glassy layer applied to the surface of a pot.

Greenware Unfired clay.

Grog A material, often clay, that has been fired to a high temperature before being added to a clay body to add strength, reduce warping and increase resistance to thermal shock.

Heatwork The combination of both heat and time and its impact on firing a glaze and clay to maturity.

Kidney A tool used to help lift the walls when throwing onto smooth surfaces.

Leather hard The state of clay after it has been shaped and dried a little. It is still wet to the touch but much firmer than when freshly thrown and can be handled with care without distorting.

Matt A glaze finish that doesn't appear glossy.

Mole The unit of weight to measure chemical amounts.

Molecular weight The weight of the atoms in the molecule.

Molecule A group of atoms chemically bonded together.

Oxidation Firing atmosphere with oxygen.

Oxide An element combined with oxygen.

Pinholing Small holes, roughly the size of a pin, that occur in the fired glaze surface – a glaze defect.

Plasticity The quality of a material that is soft and can be shaped easily when wet, without reverting back to its original shape.

Porcelain A high-firing white clay body with high kaolin content. It has low plasticity, which can make it tricky to throw with. When thrown or cast thinly it is translucent.

Primary clay Clay deposits that remain at the site of the parent material (that is, have not travelled a distance via water or erosion).

Primary flux Also known as alkali metals or R_2O, found in the first column of the periodic table. Lithium, sodium and potassium.

Prop A refractory cylinder use for supporting kiln shelves while firing.

Pugmill A piece of machinery used for mechanically blending and de-airing clay.

Pulling A technique for making handles, where the clay is pulled into shape by hand.

Pyrometer An instrument used to measure the temperature of a kiln during the firing.

Pyrometric cone A pyramid of material designed to melt and bend at specific ratios of time and heat.

Raw glazing Also known as single or once firing. Glazing and firing a ware from greenware to completion, bypassing the biscuit firing.

Reclaim The process of recycling clay discarded as part of the throwing and trimming process, back into usable clay.

Reduction Firing atmosphere where free oxygen is restricted and therefore oxygen found within the clay and glaze is sought out and affected.

Refractory A material that can withstand high temperatures without melting.

Ribs *See* also 'Kidney'.

Secondary flux Also known as alkaline earth metals or Ro, they appear in the second column of the periodic table (with the exception of zinc). Magnesium, calcium, strontium, barium and zinc.

Sedimentary clay Clays that have been transported from the site of the parent material by water, ice or wind.

Shivering A glaze defect caused by compression as opposed to tension in the glaze.

Slab building The process of making a form by hand from slabs of clay.

Slake To cause a material to crumble and sometimes heat with the addition of water.

Slip Liquid clay, often used as a 'glue' when adding handles.

Specific gravity The ratio of the density of a substance to the density of another substance, in our case, water.

Stains Pigments used to add colour to glaze recipes instead of oxides or to stain clay bodies.

Stoneware A high-firing clay body, often grey to brown in colour.

Stull Chart A graph created by R.T. Stull in 1912. It plots the SiO_2 (silica) and Al_2O_3 (alumina) levels of a glaze recipe.

Unity Molecular Formula (UMF) Also known as the Seger Formula. The proportions of a glaze recipe in molecules rather than weights. This is calculated by adding the fluxes to one, with each glass former displayed in its proportion to one molecule of flux.

Viscosity The measure of a fluid's resistance to flow.

Vitrification The process of clay particles fusing together to create a sealed surface through which water cannot penetrate.

Wedging The process of preparing clay by distributing particles and grogs evenly. It can also be used to de-air and create uniformity in the clay before throwing.

INDEX

alkali metals 93
alkaline earth metals 93
alumina 29, 94
bat wash 113
biscuit 105–107
blistering 89
bowls 22, 54–55
candling 104
celadon 110
centring 36, 42
chamois leather 42
chucks 42–43
clay 29, 30, 103
clay preparation 29–35
colour 12, 80, 95–96, 110
crawling 82, 89
crazing 81, 88, 101
cultural appropriation 17
cylinder 37–40
deflocculation 83–84
design 9–27, 80–81
distortion 51
drawing 14, 16
drying 40
durability 11, 81, 101
earthenware 106
electric kiln 111
epsom salts 83
equipment 131–132
eutectic 93
experimentation 115–123
feldspar 29
fettling 79, 128

firing 103–113
flange 26, 67
flocculation 83–84
fluxes 93, 99
flux ratio 81, 93, 100, 101
foot-ring 19, 45, 46
gas kiln 111
glaze chemistry 91–101
glazing 75–89
greenware 103
handle blanks 56–57
handles 24–25, 56–60
handles
  pulled 25, 56–60, 71
hard panning 84
health and safety 76, 131
heatwork 109
jug 62–64
kneading 32–34
  ram's head 33
  spiral 34
lids 26–27, 67–70, 71
line blends 86–87
maker's mark 20, 48
molecular weight 97
mugs 23
oxidation 110
oxides 98
pinholes 87
plaster bats 49, 117, 132–133
plasticity 29, 103
plates 21, 52–54
porcelain 30, 106

primary clay 29
prototyping 16
pug mill 31, 129
pyrometric cones 109–110
ram's head 33
raw glazing 79
raw materials 15, 94–96, 115
reclaim 49, 129
reduction 110
seaweed 118
sedimentary clay 29
Seger formula 96
shivering 88
shrinkage 21
silica 29, 94
single firing 106
slip 62, 116
slumping 54
specific gravity 76, 82, 135
spouts 24–25, 60–67, 71
stains 95
stoneware 30, 106
studio layout 125–132

Stull 88, 100–101
sustainability 10
teapot 60, 65–67, 71–73
temperature 109–110
terracotta 30
test tiles 15, 84–86
throwing bats 40, 51
throwing gauge 36, 51
tools
    glaze tools 75–76
    throwing tools 35 , 127
    trimming tools 43
trimming 41–47, 69
unity molecular formula 96–101
viscosity 82
vitrification 103–104
wax resist 80
wedging 31–32
wheel pins 52
wild clay 115–117
wood ash 117–118
wood kiln 111

First published in 2024 by
The Crowood Press Ltd
Ramsbury, Marlborough
Wiltshire SN8 2HR

enquiries@crowood.com
www.crowood.com

© Catherine and Matt West 2024

All rights reserved. No part of this publication may be reproduced or transmitted in any form or by any means, electronic or mechanical, including photocopy, recording, or any information storage and retrieval system, without permission in writing from the publishers.

British Library Cataloguing-in-Publication Data
A catalogue record for this book is available from the British Library.

ISBN 978 0 7198 4457 7

Cover design by Sergey Tsvetkov
Cover photograph by India Hobson
Frontispiece: Tableware forms in Pottery West's 'olive' glaze
(Photo: India Hobson)
Contents: Aerial view of throwing a cylinder at the wheel

Catherine and Matt West have asserted their right under the Copyright, Designs and Patents Act 1988 to be identified as the authors of this work.

Typeset by Envisage IT
Printed and bound in India by Thomson Press Ltd

DEDICATION

For Steve West